**DO NOT REMOVE
CARDS FROM POCKET**

THE INTERNATIONAL GRAIN TRADE:

PROBLEMS AND PROSPECTS

The International Grain Trade:

PROBLEMS AND PROSPECTS

Nick Butler

ST. MARTIN'S PRESS
New York

© 1986 The Royal Institute of International Affairs
All rights reserved. For information, write:
Scholarly & Reference Division,
St. Martin's Press, Inc., 175 Fifth Avenue, New York, NY 10010
First published in the United States of America in 1986
Printed in Great Britain

Library of Congress Cataloging-in-Publication Data

Butler, Nick.
     The international grain trade.

     Bibliography: p.
     Includes index.
     1. Grain trade. I. Title.
     HD9030.5.B88   1986   382′.4131   86-13768
     ISBN 0-312-42198-2

CONTENTS

2304625

LIST OF TABLES

Summary Tables

EDITORIAL STATEMENT

This study is the sixth in the Croom Helm Commodity Series. The aim of the Series is to advance the understanding of issues relating to the production and marketing of primary commodities. Most volumes in the Series, including this one, will concentrate on analysing the essential properties, production and trade of a single commodity or commodity grouping. Other volumes, in contrast – such as the fourth, *Commodity Models for Forecasting and Policy Analysis* by Walter Labys and Peter Pollack are wider in compass and are designed to draw out some general themes. Although differing markedly in content, the aim is that all volumes in the Series will share a similar form and direction, so that they may be useful for reference purposes. Similarly, each of the studies is to set the subject of commodity production firmly within the framework of the changing international economic environment and will include a prospects section. It is hoped, in consequence, that some light may be shed on the future profile of commodity production and trade and that the Series will be broad in its appeal. For, as has been illustrated by recent developments in the London Metal Exchange, the issues arising from primary commodity production and trade are far-reaching and may no longer be considered of exclusive interest to producers in developing countries.

Fiona Gordon-Ashworth
Series Editor

PREFACE

It is a pleasure rather than a duty to thank all those without whose assistance in one form or another this book could not have been produced. In particular I am grateful to Andrew Ashby, Rick Bacon, Richard Balfe, Bill Bundy, Stuart Challinor, Neil Chrimes, William Clark, David Curry, Jean-Baptiste Danel, Susanna Davies, James Eberle, Bill de Maria, Lawrence Freedman, Nicole Gallimore, Janet Gunn, Stuart Harris, Tony Jackson, John Marsh, Mark Mitchell, Peter Muriel, Robert Paarlberg, Gordon Rock, James Rollo, James Ross, Stephen Rossides, Peter Sowden, Nick Sigler, Anna Stabrawa, Alan Swinbank, Tom Walker, David Watt, William Wallace, Pauline Wickham and Catherine Wiseman. I am also grateful to those who typed the manuscript at various stages – Ann De'ath, Ruth Fay, Sally Holmes and Jean Pell. None of the above are responsible for the errors that remain, or the judgements made.

British Petroleum gave me a generous secondment in order to research and write at Chatham House, but have in no way sought to control the output. My gratitude is due to them, as is a confirmation of the fact that what follows is a personal and not a corporate view.

This book is written in the ambitious hope that it can illuminate some of the current problems of international agricultural trade and that reason as well as charity can do something to assist those, in many countries of the world, who do not have the benefit of regular and adequate nutrition. This book is dedicated to them.

Nick Butler

1 INTRODUCTION

Like clothes or popular music, political issues, however serious, are vulnerable to the fluctuating tides of fashion and to the shortness of the span of public attention. Ten years ago the food crisis was an issue in fashion. Commissions, task forces, research institutes, charitable bodies, diplomats and politicians were all involved. A dozen new institutions to analyse the problem of food security and agricultural development were set up within a period of less than three years. A World Food Conference was convened in Rome, provoking a bureaucratic contest in Washington as to whether the State Department or the Department of Agriculture was to lead the American delegation. Henry Kissinger, who won the contest, committed the United States to work for policies which would ensure that by 1985 'no child in the world would go to bed hungry'. As a consequence of the rise in prices in 1972 and 1973, the Soviet decision to purchase grain on the world market instead of relying solely on domestic supplies, and the American decision to limit exports in order to protect domestic consumers in a period of rising inflation, insecurity of supply appeared to be a permanent feature of the world food trade, affecting all importers, especially those least able to pay the demanded price, or to store reserve stocks as insurance.

In the frantic search for countervailing leverage after the assertion of OPEC's influence in the winter of 1973/4, food power became an object of active discussion and advocacy in the United States. Exporters of a scarce commodity, in this case grain, must according to the simple logic employed at the time have a corresponding power to grant or deny supplies. Despite the powerful intellectual demolition work done by Emma Rothschild and others,[1] food power retained its attractions until its use and dramatic failure when an embargo on grain supplies was imposed after the Soviet invasion of Afghanistan.

By that time the issue of security of supply, born of fears of absolute shortage and a shortage artificially created by the exercise of food power, had lost its fashionable appeal as well. Years of good harvests, the introduction of stability to the Soviet-American

1

relationship and the depressant effect of recession on demand took food from the headlines, and from the pages of all but a few academic journals.

There is another element to be considered in examining why food supply attracted so much attention in the 1970s. The years after 1973 were the age of the forecaster. The oil crisis caused every business and every government to consider the outlook for years ahead. The 1975 recession ended years of growth in which the need to plan for anything other than continuing expansion appeared unnecessary. Suddenly the supply of basic necessities appeared uncertain – not just for political reasons, such as the Arab embargo on oil exports, but also because of physical limits. The adjective 'finite' became inseparable from the noun 'resources'. Long-term projections typically involved graphics with two diverging lines of demand and supply — the former usually well above the latter as the date on the bottom axis approached 2000. The simple equations based on population growth, per capita consumption requirements and physically limited supply showed unsurprisingly that by the end of the century, if not sooner, the world would have too little oil, wood, land and food. As one forecaster put it at the time, 2001 would be closer to the stone age than to the sort of world Stanley Kubrik had imagined.

In the mid-1980s it all looks remarkably different. For almost all the key traded commodities prices are at or near ten- or twenty-year lows reflecting an underlying imbalance of supply — pushed up in many instances by technical advance — and effective demand, demand, that is to say, backed by the purchasing power required to produce or import. A decade of recession, and low growth has restricted and stunted that effective demand.

But recession alone is an insufficient explanation of why the forecasts of the 1970s now look so unconvincing. In the case of food, and to some degree in relation to many other commodities, forecasters assumed that the world market was a single entity. In grain at least reality does not match that assumption. Instead there exists a two-tier market — between different countries and also within individual countries, particularly in the Third Word. The trading sector comprises the main exporters of grain and a variety of developed and developing country importers, including now most of the centrally planned nations of the Communist bloc, while the non-trading sector accounts for those communities — nations, regions, villages — which scrape an existence without recourse to the purchase of any agricultural goods which they themselves do not produce. For them, the choice of self-sufficiency is not a deliberate, political one, but rather a choice imposed by economic necessity. The absence of purchasing power keeps hundreds of millions of individuals away from the markets which could supply their needs. Even those Third World countries which do import grain on a regular basis and in growing amounts use it to supply only a fraction of their populations, usually the urbanised minority. Rural communities have little or no link with the world market and huge though their potential needs undoubtedly are, they go un-fulfilled whether the United States and Europe have surpluses or not.

The trading market has undoubtedly expanded in the last decade but it still accounts for perhaps no more than 60 per cent of the world's population. The extent to which that figure is maintained or increased must be one of the key questions for any forecast. The scale of actual participation in the markets will probably be the crucial factor conditioning future price levels and determining the fortunes of the farm sector in western developed countries.

For the moment the trading sector of the market finds itself in the depths of a recession which no one anticipated a decade ago. Stocks of wheat and coarse grain continue to rise even after an exceptional withdrawal of American land from production in 1983. World prices in real terms are at levels unseen since the 1950s. In the United States where farmers lack much of the financial protection available to their European cousins there is serious talk of farm poverty and of bankruptcy arising from debt, reminiscent of the worst of the scenes of the 1930s described by Steinbeck. The expansion of man's ability to produce has not been matched by the development of man's ability to manage the economy of the world in ways which would permit the efficient distribution of that production. Though there is a flow of concessionary and free food in aid, the trickle of charity has solved neither the problems of supply, and the suppliers, nor those of demand, and the hungry.

This book is not intended as a further contribution to the growing literature, some of it of very high quality, on the food needs and agricultural problems of the non-trading half of the world. Its aim instead is to examine and to try to explain how the grain market works and how it might develop. Though the emphasis is therefore on the developed countries, the analysis and the history of the last few years demonstrate clearly that just as a divided and partial world market contributes to the current set of problems, so an extension of that market can offer a contribution to their solution.

The Economies of the Grain Trade

As a business, grain is difficult to reconcile with the smooth logical mechanisms of trade as described by the economic textbooks. Costs are certainly lower in the United States than in Europe, but it has been Europe which has consistently expanded its production in the last two decades. Nor does the imbalance of supply and demand in the trading sector have the effect on output which the standard assumptions would lead one to expect. Production has continued to grow in volume even when prices have been low and falling. Though unit production costs have dropped as a consequence of technical advances, that fall in itself has been far from sufficient to compensate for the fall in prices.

If the grain market is determined by something more than simply the balance of supply and demand, it cannot be mistaken for a cartel. There are a limited number of exporters to the world market — the United States, the EEC, Canada, Australia and Argentina — but no agreement on either floor prices (below which grain would not be sold) or quotas (dividing the world market between the five). In the absence of either, competition for markets in times of surplus is fierce and contributes itself to the weakness of trading prices. Five trading firms dominate the flow of grain around the world, but they appear to exercise little influence over prices.

Instead of a hidden hand, as defined by Adam Smith, there is an open hand offering a fistful of dollars, francs, pounds or Deutschmarks as export subsidies. Competitive protectionism is the dominant characteristic of the grain market, its influence extending over the last two decades to affect not just the domestic markets of the countries concerned but also the world market. The international grain trade has become by default the buffer between the decisions of national governments, absorbing the strain of fluctuations in national supply or demand. European policy using variable levies as a means of controlling the influence of trade on domestic producers and consumers is the clearest example but almost all countries to one degree or another have sought protection from variations of supply levels or price in the international market.

Apart from the very special case of the defence industries (in economic terms a public good, not a trading industry), agriculture has received more support consistently across countries with a wide range of political systems (many of them inherently hostile to public sector interventionism) than any other single sector of the economy. For those not familiar with agriculture, this always comes as a surprise and requires some explanation. Concern with security of supply — the risks that war will restrict trade routes and that the flow of food necessary to feed armies and peoples will be halted — has long obsessed those countries whose economies and territories do not in normal circumstances (i.e., without subsidy) produce adequate indigenous supplies. A concern with security of supply in this sense is nothing new, but can be traced back to the concern with import dependence expressed by the rulers of the medieval city states, and to even earlier times.

Even in an age of trade and open supply, with shi ¿ping routes probably as secure as they have ever been, the concern has remained. Few countries are prepared to trust the provision of a basic commodity to others.

Mixed with that concern go two other factors — one economic and one political. In economic terms agriculture has won support as the disadvantaged section of rapidly growing industrial economies. Productivity developments, economies of scale and changing patterns of demand have shifted wealth to the urban, industrial economy at the expense of the rural sector, with its instabilities of climate and of crops, its high fixed costs, and its low returns on investment. Though recession and the effects of financial support for the CAP may have concealed that effect in Britain in recent years, no analysis can ignore the desire to balance town and country as a motivation of central government economic policy in any modern industrial economy. In Japan, rice prices are subsidised not to encourage the production of yet more rice but to support the income levels of the rice farmers in particular areas which would otherwise rest at a subsistence level unacceptable in a prosperous advanced economy. The pattern is repeated in France, Britain, West Germany and the United States. Even strong measures of farm income support, such as the CAP, have failed to eliminate the differential. In France, statistics just produced show the French farmer remaining a poor relative to his cousins in industry. Income may be higher under the CAP than it was forty years ago and land values may be increasing, but absolute earning levels are still below those in car production or computer software or the public sector.

The increase in land values may have permitted borrowing, but the increasing capital value can only be realised if the land, the farmer's basic capital asset, is sold.[2]

The political factor is relevant, and is probably more complex than the simple model, which sees only the massed ranks of farmers gathered in the National Farmers Union, or the American Farm Bureau or the French farm organisations, would suggest. As a whole the rural community has lost population but not political strength. Political structures have been slow to reflect migration trends, and rural areas, whether in France or the United States, still command a disproportionate share of political influence. Britain, with its regular boundary commission reports shifting the geography of parliamentary seats to match the flow of people, is probably less susceptible to this than many other developed countries. In the United States, jealously protected rights of the individual states have maintained much of the original construction of the Constitution. As reported in chapter 2, 30 senators come from farm states. In France rural constituencies are still crucial in any election, and no French government can go too far in offending rural interests, of which the farmers' lobby is by far the best organised. For many years the influence of the minority parties in successive West German coalitions has institutionalised the support for relatively high farm prices within the European Community expressed through the policies and speeches of such farm ministers as Dr Josef Ertl, from the Free Democrats, and his successor Herr Ignaz Kiechle from the CSU. With over 80 per cent of all grain production consumed within the boundaries of the producing countries the political decision to support the farm sector might appear to be of marginal importance in international terms. Protectionism in general, however, and the specific form which it has taken in the last few years, has had the effect of making even more unstable the flow of trade, which in a sector vulnerable to climate and disease is inherently susceptible to fluctuations. Protection transfers most, if not all, of that instability on to the 17 per cent or so of world grain output which is traded internationally and thus to the countries dependent on that trade for a significant proportion of their supplies or income. Ten years ago that instability was described in terms of the dangers of rising prices forcing the poorer importers out of the market. Now it can be seen more clearly in the export of surpluses by the EEC regardless of the price depressant effect on other exporters.

With the secure boundary fence of variable levies, none of the price effect in either direction finds its way back to the European producer. Without price signals from the market, only the politically determined price judgements of the European farm ministers exist to indicate to farmers what should or should not be produced.

The evidence of the last few years is that the farm ministers' conclusions are more likely to reflect a balancing of interests between the farm sectors of the various member states (and between various groups within the agricultural sector) than a balance of supply and demand.

The grain market is therefore an issue of importance which goes beyond intellectual curiosity or any general concern over the misallocation of resources which excessive subsidy and protection implies. Though less than a fifth of output is traded, that trade represents a vital interest for both exporters and importers. The United States has earned over $20 billion in each of the last three years from agricultural exports, the bulk of them grain, which alone has balanced 2 million barrels per day of oil imports. The Chinese imported 13 million tons of grain in 1983, to supply the cities of the coast, and the armies stationed on the northern border with the Soviet Union. Australia and Canada rely on grain production for export as a means of sustaining many rural communities in both countries. The Soviet Union, regularly importing 30 million tons a year and in the 1984/5 crop year over 50 million tons, may only buy 5–10 per cent of its annual needs from outside, but even that small percentage is crucial if the alternative is a small cut in supplies to either the makers of bread or the farmers of livestock.

Over the last decade the importance of trade has spread further. In the Middle East in particular the oil states and their neighbours in Jordan, Syria and Egypt have increased imports of grain to feed their growing populations. Apart from Egypt, the trade has been generally commercial, rather than concessionary, funded by oil and economic growth, and it has become an accepted feature of economic life, and of daily existence, almost a requirement which if unfulfilled would threaten political stability.

This range of involvement makes all the more important the organisation of a market which is expected to meet such a variety of needs. Without effective organisation the instability of the market, magnified by the impact of protection, can jeopardise any of the interests involved to an extent quite out of proportion to the actual shift in supply involved. No market can (or should) be immune to change or instability, but the chance that change will worsen an already precarious and unstable situation should be a cause for concern, particularly if the instability threatens to add to the problems of destitution and hunger in the world, or to poison the international climate, and the relatively open and harmonious trading relations built up since the war.

This book is part description, part forecast and part prescription. There is inevitably some overlap between one section and another, but the lines of demarcation are, I hope, reasonably clear. Wishful thinking has not been allowed to penetrate the forecast, not least because the international climate still appears to be hostile to the imposition of organised management. For the time being the mood is perhaps still better illustrated by Dr Milton Friedman's call for the abolition of the International Monetary Fund, on the grounds that it was in danger of becoming a world central bank. But that, too, may reflect no more than a passing fashion; intellectual hemlines may rise again and time may provide new opportunities for efforts to manage the international system in rational ways. Excessive pessimism would be as misplaced as would an expression of the false optimism which sees an overarching network of international organisations as the final managerial solution to all problems.

Since the world market is the residual creation of national policies, the book begins by examining those national policies in some detail, concentrating on the recent history and immediate circumstances of the three main actors — the United States, the EEC and the USSR. In each, the progress of events has transformed essentially domestic policies designed to deal with domestic problems into actions with international consequences. The United States — with a massive agricultural capacity and with an economic system which encourages innovation and the use of the most efficient technology as well as providing the flows of capital for such change — has found since the 1950s that domestic demand in almost all but the most exceptional crop years is easily outstripped by supply. The world market, whether in the form of a hungry Europe after the Second World War, the destitute of the Third World, political allies in Viet Nam and Egypt, or commercial customers from Moscow to Seoul, has offered the natural solution. For the EEC, by contrast, the world market has, until recently, been something to be avoided — a source of cheaper supplies than most European farmers can produce which did not suit the European judgement that indigenous agriculture should be supported and sustained from public funds for regional, social and political reasons. Once a matter of concern only to domestic consumers and taxpayers, the policy has gradually come to involve first those countries whose trade was gradually eliminated from European markets, and, more recently, those whose markets in third countries are under threat from the European disposal of surpluses as the barrier of self-sufficiency within the EEC was first reached and then surmounted.

For the Soviet Union, also, involvement in the international market is a consequence of domestic policy. The failings of Soviet agriculture — once a supplier of the world market, including Britain — forced the Soviet leadership in the 1970s to confront the choice of limiting still further available supplies of bread and meat to their own population or sacrificing the principle of strategic self-sufficiency entrenched since 1917. They chose and appear to be sticking to the latter course, regularly importing on a significant scale each year, and minimising the sense of dependence only by seeking to draw supplies from a variety of sources and not from any single exporter.

Chapters 5 and 6 deal with the way in which the agricultural trading systems and the grain trade in particular are organised. Agriculture has never been subjected to the practice of an open trading system as established by GATT and has remained exempt from most of the Treaty's clauses. Management (or cartelisation, as its critics would say), whether through the International Wheat Council or through the other agencies, has fared no better, though it has been attempted on half a dozen occasions since the war. Fears about insecurity of supply in the 1970s generated new organisations, but neither the efforts to establish secure reserves for use in times of crisis, or the hopes of spreading agricultural technology and the most modern farming techniques to the Third World, have experienced dramatic success. The most successful organisations have been the research bodies — such as CIMMYT in Mexico on the technical side and the International Food Policy Research Institute in Washington on the economic. Neither, though, would claim that their work is sufficient to encompass let alone solve all the problems involved.

Chapter 6, by Susanna Davies, looks at the institutions which, in the absence of international control, have managed the market — the international grain trading companies, fascinatingly private but more concerned with profit and margins than with control. The companies are the grease in the cogs of the international grain market, and though some of their decision making determines the shape of that market they are less all-powerful than some conspiracy theorists would suggest. Privacy, however, has kept researchers at bay, and there is still much work to be done in defining the shape and extent of commercial influence in the otherwise uncontrolled system.

Chapter 7 looks at the development and the consequences to date of one of the trade disputes which an uncontrolled system has produced. The conflict for markets between US and European producers has contributed to the deterioration of trade relations, and while the issue has been put aside during the past two years as a consequence of the American decision to take land out of production, the longer-term problem remains unresolved. The involvement of government in the form of the EEC Commission and the US Department of Agriculture has complicated rather than eased the difficulties of negotiating a solution. The US-European dispute is of course not the only issue of conflict arising from agricultural trade. The dispute between US exporters and the aggressively protectionist Japanese also reflects the pressures created by surplus on the one hand and the political strength of the lobby to defend farming interests on the other. It has been described in detail in a recently published study.[3]

The subsequent chapters examine those regions whose economic circumstances and political choices will determine the direction of the market for the future.

For Europe the chances of significant reform of the CAP look slim. The budget crisis now facing the Community can be solved in a number of ways, many of them producing no more than marginal reform and leaving current structures pretty much intact. The assumption must be that in any anticipation of the future market the odds are on continuing European surpluses if not a formal export policy. To other exporters the chance of escaping from an era of low prices then depends not just upon the question of which developing countries remain within or join the trading system, but also on their attitudes and policies if and when they do join. The final two chapters consider those countries which by virtue of the combination of population growth and economic success offer the potential markets of the future. Between them, countries in South East Asia offer a market of over 1,500 million people, few of whom at present consume significant quantities of grain either directly as a staple part of the diet or indirectly through the consumption of meat reared on grain-based animal feeds. To conclude that an economically open China, and a prosperous South East Asia will in ten or twenty years have taken up the slack in the world market and will have pushed up total demand to match (or even outstrip) supply would be too glib and insensitive to the real risk that the uncertainties of an insecure market will persist in the long run.

Notes

1. Emma Rothschild, 'Food Politics', *Foreign Affairs*, January 1976 and Robert Paarlberg, 'Lessons of the Grain Embargo', *Foreign Affairs*, Fall 1980.

2. For a commentary on the effects of the recession on farm incomes see *The Agricultural Situation in the Community, 1983*, published by the European Commission. The table below sets out the Commission's estimate of the farm income index (the index of net value added by agriculture at factor cost per person employed, in real terms).

1973	105.7
1974	96.3
1975	97.9
1976	100.2
1977	99.0
1978	101.2
1979	98.9
1980	92.6
1981	92.4
1982	100.7

3. *US Japanese Agricultural Trade Relations*, Resources for the Future, Washington DC, 1982

2 THE UNITED STATES

In less than thirty years the agricultural sector of the US economy has been transformed from a relatively labour-intensive and domestically orientated accumulation of individual farm operations to a major export industry characterised by concentration of ownership and a capital-intensive production technology.

From a peak of almost 7,000,000 in the mid-1930s, the total number of farm units had declined to 5,600,000 by 1950 and to 2,600,000 by 1980. The total area farmed, however, allowing for year to year variations, remained around 380 million acres (some 20 per cent of the land area of the USA), and it has been the development of ever larger farms rather than any cut in land usage which has transformed the industry. The largest 25 per cent of US farms now account for 85 per cent of all sales.[1]

With the increase in average size has come a concentration of ownership — away from the individual farmer or family business to corporate control — and an even more significant decline in the workforce. In 1950 some 15 billion man-hours were devoted to farm work. By the mid-1970s the figure was down to 5 billion and by 1982 to little more than 4 billion. The agricultural labour force has fallen by 60 per cent since 1920, and the farm population by 80 per cent. The rural population as a whole has declined from 45 per cent of US citizens to 25 per cent.

Within agriculture, the substitution of capital for labour, with the amount of land used remaining static, has been the main factor behind the sharp increase in labour productivity. Table 2.1 shows the trend over 60 years.

The reasons for these changes and consequent achievements of the United States in improving yields and output to the extent that she has been able to become a key supplier of world markets, are complex. Inflation has increased the attractiveness of land as an asset, pushing up prices and thereby expanding the borrowing and investment capacity of farmers. New technology has been readily accessible and the adaptation process relatively easy. Some technology — four-wheel-drive tractors, electronic harvesting equipment and computerised crop-monitoring — has contributed to

Table 2.1: The US Farm Sector Output and Productivity Indices
(1950 = 100)

| | Output | | | | Productivity | | |
	Total	Total grains	Feed grain	Food grain	Total farm output (per unit of total input)	Crop production per acre	Farm output per hour of farm work
1929	72	81	75	80	74	81	47
1960	125	122	135	135	126	131	195
1970	138	131	139	141	143	149	347
1980	169	171	190	247	164	168	589
1981	193	197	237	294	190	192	689
1982	187	200	243	286	187	197	689
1983	152	147	131	237	161	168	621
1984	179	186	222	261	179	190	684

Source: USDA, *Economic Indicators of the Farm Sector. Production and Efficiency Statistics*, 1985.

the shift to larger-scale farms. Two decades of significant expansion of the US economy allowed a relatively painless shift from employment in the farm sector and encouraged the substitution of capital for labour.

With grain and food consumption in general in the United States growing only slowly, the farm sector has been dependent for its prosperity and expansion on foreign sales, supported through much of the period by price guarantees from the US government. These support measures have helped US farmers to trade at world market prices but have never been so comprehensive or extensive as those offered by the EEC.

The effect on the industry of both technological change and the support system has been to increase its dependence on the external market.

As the structure of farming has changed, so too has the pattern of production, in response to fluctuations and opportunities in world markets. Food and feed grains along with soyabeans have dominated the expansion of US agricultural output. Table 2.2 shows the volume index of output for grain and other agricultural products.

The growth in output and land values meant that by the 1970s farms had in general become profitable concerns with rates of return and capital gains comparable to those of other sectors. From

Table 2.2: Farm Production Indices (1977 = 100)

	1950	1960	1975	1985
Total farm production	61	76	95	117
Livestock	70	82	95	110
Crops	59	72	93	117
Feedgrains	51	69	91	132
Foodgrains	49	66	108	120

Table 2.3: Farm Income and Debt

	Net farm income		Total farm debt
	Current $	1967 $	
1970	14.4	12.4	53.0
1975	25.6	15.9	81.6
1978	27.4	14.0	122.7
1979	31.7	14.6	140.8
1980	21.2	8.2	165.8
1981	29.8	11.0	182.0
1982	24.6	8.5	217.2
1983	15.0	5.0	216.3
1984	34.5	11.1	212.5

Source: USDA, *Agricultural Finance. Outlook and Situation Report*, 1985.

the mid-1960s to the end of the 1970s 'total returns to farm investment equity substantially exceeded investments in common stocks and bonds'.[2] Now, though, the industry is far from healthy. Structural change has not brought stability. The last three years have seen successive waves of bankruptcies as farmers have found themselves unable to meet the cost of servicing or repaying the debts accumulated in the previous decade. Table 2.3 shows how the problem has developed with farm income too low to service debt incurred in the purchase of land.

The decline in the growth of the net farm debt in the mid 1980s is more an indicator of weakness than of refound strength. Banks and others have grown more reluctant to lend, as real farm income has fallen and as the prospects for recovery have faded. Farm debt outstanding finally stabilised in 1983 as a result of the Payment in Kind programme. A 19 per cent reduction in planted acreage of major crops produced a sharp fall in expenditure of inputs,[3] though the reduction in scale of the PIK programme after its first year of operation renewed the problem and brought a wave of bankruptcies among both farmers and bankers in the early months of 1985. With total debt at $210 billion the problem is being aggravated by a sharp fall in land values. According to a USDA study published in June 1985, the value of farmland fell by 12 per cent on average, and by 25 per cent in the corn belt in just twelve months from April 1984 to April 1985. The farm sector as a whole is now in the unfortunate position of living on credit which present market conditions do not justify. It is an unhappy conclusion to a period of major advance in technology and productivity.

In macroeconomic terms the role of the agricultural sector within the American economy has shifted radically over the last three decades but the shift has if anything increased its importance. The figures on man-hours quoted above demonstrate the decline of agriculture as a source of direct employment. Even in the areas commonly designated as farm states, the farm workforce has shrunk rapidly. The related industries — transportation, processing and marketing — remain, but the overall number of individuals dependent on agriculture for their livelihood has declined, perhaps by as much as 50 per cent.

Agriculture's contribution to GNP, however, has declined more slowly and remains substantial. Taking into account the related industries, agriculture is a key element in the economic prosperity of whole regions and numerous states. In the period of slow growth since the mid-1970s the role of agriculture in national output has stabilised, as it has outperformed other industries.

In balance of payments terms the positive contribution of agriculture, and specifically grain, is relatively recent. Though agriculture represents only 3 per cent of GDP, it now accounts for almost a fifth of all US exports. Table 2.4 below shows the trends, in opposite directions, of the US overall trade balance, and the balance in the agricultural sector as well as the importance of grain sales.

The devaluation of the dollar at the beginning of the 1970s paved the way for the establishment of a major grain exporting industry.

Internationally the effect of the rapid expansion of US output has been to increase the share of US exports in world markets. Table 2.5 illustrates this trend and also the extent to which it has been reversed in the last three years.

The balance of payments gains, helping to offset the adverse oil trade balance of the mid to late 1970s, were a direct consequence of the trend. Just as many parts of the world are now reliant on supplies of US grain, the US is equally dependent — nationally as well as

Table 2.4: The US Trade Balance

US bn $		Exports		Imports		Balance
	Total	Agricultural	Grains	Total	Oil	
1965	26.5	6.3	3.7	21.5	2.0	+5.0
1970	42.5	7.4	4.4	39.9	2.9	+2.6
1975	107.1	22.2	15.9	98.2	27.0	+8.9
1980	224.3	42.1	27.1	249.8	79.3	−25.5
1981	237.1	44.0	28.6	265.1	78.0	−28.0
1982	211.2	37.2	23.4	247.7	61.3	−36.5
1983	201.7	37.2	23.4	268.9	55.0	−67.2
1984	219.9	38.3	24.0	334.0	57.5	−114.1

Source: Economic Report of the President. US Government, February, 1986.
Figures for grain include oilseeds.

Table 2.5: The US Share of World Grain Trade

	1970/71	74/75	79/80	80/81	81/82	82/83	83/84	84/85	85/86
Wheat									
World trade	54.3	63.4	86.0	93.0	99.3	96.1	100.4	103.9	88
US exports	19.8	28.3	36.6	42.1	49.3	39.3	38.3	38.0	26
US share of trade (%)	36	45	51	45	50	41	38	37	29
Coarse grain									
World trade	48.8	59.7	98.2	100.5	101.5	88.0	89.9	101.9	88
US exports	19.5	34.6	71.6	72.4	61.4	52.9	55.5	58.4	46
US share of trade (%)	40	58	73	72	61	60	62	57	52

Source: International Wheat Council, *Market Report*, various issues.
Figures for 1985/86 are estimates

directly in the farm states — on grain sales. The figures for exports
as a percentage of production vary from grain to grain (from 28 per
cent for feed grains in general, to 34 per cent for maize and 57 per
cent for wheat), but the trend has been generally upwards, with
three-quarters of the increase in grain output since the early 1960s
accounted for by exports. Exports generated a quarter of all farm
receipts by 1980 against only 10 per cent thirty years earlier. For
grain producers, of course, the figure was even higher. Export
markets have conditioned not only the shift in the pattern of
production in favour of maize and soyabeans but have also had an
important impact on subsidiary transport sectors, including the rail
and port network on both the east and west coasts. It is not

surprising therefore that the impact of a deteriorating export market has been painful and expensive.

The development of an export market for grain began as, and remains, the consequence of the divergence of the trends of supply and demand within the US. While supply of grain and the efficiency of its production increased with technical progress and the spread of intensively mechanised farming methods, demand has grown only slowly and has now virtually plateaued. The consumption of bread, and other grain-based products has reached a natural limit, while increases in meat consumption have been met by increases in the efficiency of feed use, and by a shift in demand from beef to chicken; total feed demand has accordingly remained almost static.

The divergence of the two trends poses the central problem for the makers of US agricultural policy. Without government intervention in the market farm returns would be very low, and the income of the farm sector and the dependent rural community well below income levels in other sectors, particularly given the general prosperity which has characterised the US economy. Although the emotional hold of the farm sector and the numerical weight of its population have both declined, its political importance remains considerable.

The shift in population over the last sixty years has not been matched by a shift in the mechanics of the US political system. Over 30 senators, and almost 200 congressmen out of a total of 435, still come from what can normally be defined as farm states. In the electoral college which formally elects the President, over 35 per cent of the votes are cast by representatives of the farm states out of the total of 538. The figures are only a little lower than they were fifty years ago. Beyond the core of farm states a number of other regions have significant and well-organised farm lobbies. Although population movement has taken individuals out of the agricultural sector, the absence of any clear alternative economic activity in the farm states has sustained the argument for federal government support for the agricultural sector even through periods of chronic surplus. The policy response to the economic conditions of the farm sector has varied considerably over the last three decades.

The problem of surplus production, with its inevitable downward pressure on prices began to be apparent in the early 1950s, as the period of post-war crisis came to an end. For a time in the post-war period, a revival of the European market provided an outlet for increasing US output.

Table 2.6: Per Capita Food Consumption in the USA (1970 = 100)

	1960	1970	1975	1981
Beef	75	100	104	92
Chicken	69	100	99	128
Total meat	90	100	94	92
Butter	142	100	89	81
Wheat flour	106	100	103	105
Cornmeal	91	100	101	100
Total Food	95	100	99	100
Population (millions)	179	203	214	226

Source: Based on USDA, *Food Consumption. Prices and Expenditure*, 1983.

The early attempt to meet the problem through disposal of surpluses to countries in particular need while farm incomes were secured by price supports proved insufficient to meet the scale of the problem. Production continued to expand and the cost, both of the PL480 programme and of price supports, to grow. (Public Law 480 gave the government the power to make donations of food, in particular grain, to countries in need.) During the Eisenhower administration the executive branch pressed for lower price supports to discourage production and to encourage flagging consumption. In defiance of the economic logic of the proposition, Congress saw this as an attack on the farming sector and voted instead to maintain support at relatively high levels, thereby further stimulating output. Only at the end of the 1950s were the first cuts made in support prices; they came too late, and were too limited to halt the process of expansion in an industry which was achieving significant savings in the unit cost of its output with every passing year.

The Kennedy Administration inherited the problem but was no more successful in finding a solution. Efforts to introduce strict supply management controls not just on grain but on most farm output met a further congressional block. Congress, despite the persistence of a serious imbalance in the market, 'maintained its adherence to voluntarism', and to the withdrawal of land by farmers only in response to inducements.

The congressional block on the administration's proposals to force land out of production was resolved only with:

a series of costly voluntary programmes designed to limit crop production and to gradually reduce all price supports to or below world market levels. With this transition virtually completed by 1964 farm incomes were maintained at politically acceptable levels by direct payments . . . The basic concepts . . . price support levels related to the market . . . income support through direct payment . . . and voluntary methods of achieving supply management remained essentially unchanged in the Farm Acts of 1965, 1970, 1973 and 1977.[4]

For the next decade the problem was solved by the unexpectedly rapid expansion of export trade. The farming industry moved to yet higher levels of output in the confident belief that economic growth, and a rising world population would provide an effective long-term commercial market. The sharpest increase came in the early 1970s. Fuelled by the devaluation of the dollar, which made American exports competitive to an extent unknown in the 1960s, by the Soviet decision to meet its requirements by importing, and by a sustained drive for new markets in the more prosperous of the developing countries, American exports grew by 140 per cent in volume terms between 1968 and 1973. Their value showed a still higher growth as volume increases coincided with the tight market conditions of the time.

The confidence that the United States had discovered a new and growing export industry led to an inflow of new capital and an extension of borrowing for modernisation and expansion. The boom, however, was short-lived. A strengthening of the dollar hindered the export market and by the end of the Ford Administration government was having to confront the problem of renewed and increasing surpluses, coupled with falling world market prices which by 1976 were back at the 1970 level. In constant dollars, net farm operator income declined by 60 per cent between 1973 and 1976 — to a level as low as that of 1940.

The agricultural legislation of 1977 reiterated the principles of voluntary set aside programmes and direct income supports. The main innovation was a farmer-owned reserve funded by government which aimed to keep prices up by taking grain out of the market.

The evidence is that over the period from 1977 to 1980 the farmer-owned reserve achieved its principal objective, with the assistance of favourable external conditions. Stocks, to meet future fluctuations in supply or demand, were increased. A recent and authoritative study of the subject shows a 4.5 per cent increase in wheat stocks and a still higher growth of corn stocks even taking into account stocks outside the reserve.[5] Storage capacity expanded and the government's ability to control the market was enhanced. Grain prices were undoubtedly higher than they would have been without the reserve, though after the early 1970s few farmers regarded the years from 1977 to 1980 as a period of prosperity.

The major problem, however, was that the cost of the various agricultural programmes was growing, and there was no sign that the reserve could be anything other than a permanent feature of US agricultural policy.

The aim of the incoming Reagan Administration was to reduce the mounting budget cost of the farm commodity programmes. The expensive voluntary acreage reduction programme was to be restricted and the emphasis placed on the reserve, on the opening up of world markets, and finally on moderate support levels as the most appropriate means of achieving a sustainable balance.

Success has eluded the Administration. Record grain yields, a weakening and more competitive export market, and the failure of voluntary acreage reduction schemes combined to add to the reserve, which stood at over 120 million tons by the end of 1982, and coupled with the growing burden imposed on farmers by rising real interest rates forced the government into income support costing as much as $20 billion for the agricultural sector as a whole in the 1982/3 financial year — many times the original budget target.[6] Even with such a level of spending, falling prices meant continuing reductions in real farm income. The most recent attempt to stabilise the market was the Payment in Kind scheme, introduced in January 1983. Having voluntarily abandoned hope of increasing exports to absorb the accumulated surplus, the Administration devised a scheme which would reward the farmer who took land out of production by a payment of grain from the reserve stocks. Production and stocks would both fall, and in the medium term prices would rise as a new equilibrium was achieved.

The reduction in land cropped, which was additional to that set aside under programmes previously in place, remained voluntary and based on heavy cash inducements rather than compulsion. As Table 2.7 shows the effect of the generous inducements offered in 1983 was considerable.

Nevertheless, the Payment in Kind programme could not provide a permanent solution. A rundown of the very substantial level of stocks is certainly desirable but as the farm lobby has been quick to

Table 2.7:　US Grain Production (million tons)

	1981	1982	1983	1984	1985 (estimate)
Wheat	76.0	76.4	65.9	70.6	66.0
Feed grains of which	248.4	255.0	136.0	236.9	273.8
Maize	208.3	213.3	105.8	194.9	225.2
Barley	10.4	11.4	11.1	13.0	12.8
Oats	7.4	9.0	6.9	6.9	7.5
Sorghum	22.4	21.4	12.2	22.0	28.3
Soyabeans	54.4	62.0	42.6	50.6	57.1

Source: International Wheat Council, *Market Report*, various issues.

point out it does nothing to raise farm income, unless prices rise, and by taking up to a third of land out of production it posed severe problems for the agricultural supply industry, and the rural community whose livelihood depends on providing farm needs.

Though the PIK programme was of some value in reducing the level of stocks as shown by Table 2.8, the achievement was limited by the fact that farmers maximise their output from the best land, leaving only the least productive fallow. The programme's limited duration also reduced its effectiveness.

After one very expensive year (costing $6 billion in cash payments and $9 billion in payments in kind in the form of government controlled commodities) financial pressures associated with the huge federal deficit and the impact of a major drought in some producing regions forced a substantial modification of the 1984 programme.[7] The result was a sharp rebound in production

Table 2.8:　Closing Stock Levels (million tons)

End of crop year	81/82	82/83	83/84	84/85	85/6 (estimated)
Wheat	31.7	41.9	38.1	38.8	51.4
Feed grains of which	73.0	106.9	31.5	50.0	114.3
Maize	60.1	87.2	18.4	35.1	90.6
Barley	3.2	4.9	4.1	5.4	7.6
Oats	2.2	3.3	2.6	2.6	2.4
Sorghum	7.4	11.4	6.4	6.9	13.7
Soyabeans	7.3	12.4	4.8	8.6	13.3

Source: International Wheat Council, *Market Report*, various issues, based on USDA returns.

volumes, as shown in Table 2.7.

Once again, secure and indeed growing export markets came to be seen by the Administration as well as by farmers and traders as essential if the balance of supply and demand at present levels of output is to be stabilised.

The Making of US Agricultural Policy

Although as a recent study of the role of interest groups in American policy making shows, 'The general farm groups have been divided, often dogmatic and of surprisingly little effectiveness' with much of their effort concentrated on the provision of services rather lobbying, farm interests in the widest sense have been central to the process of agricultural policy making through the US Department of Agriculture and the Congress for many years.

I.M. Destler has summed up the situation which existed in the 1950s, 1960s and early 1970s:

> Farm policy concerns had primacy until 1972. Food policy-making was centred in the Department of Agriculture; its impacts on other policy concerns were largely by-products of actions taken to strengthen farm income and bring the domestic 'farm problem' under control . . . The farm problem was chronic surpluses and low prices. A remarkable technological revolution had generated dramatic productivity increases. The leap in production depressed prices because it exceeded growth of commercial demand — domestic and worldwide.[8]

However, their unfettered influence has been restrained by other considerations over the last decade.

External circumstances, and in particular economic pressures, have modified that situation. Recurrent budget pressures have forced upon successive Administrations unpalatable choices on the scale and direction of farm support. Inflationary pressures and the desire to reduce the cost of living have led governments to interfere in the operations of the grain market at moments such as in 1973 when the American consumer appeared to be threatened by rising prices as grain was exported to meet international demand. The rise in the balance of payments cost of oil imports in the mid to late 1970s forced the Administration to appreciate the value of farm exports not just as a means of disposing of surplus output, but also as a positive contribution to a deteriorating overall balance of payments.

Macro-economic considerations did not work consistently in any one direction. The burden of public expenditure going on farm price supports led politicians and bureaucrats in the Department of Agriculture, not to mention farmers and the grain companies, to argue for a policy of commercial exports without restriction. Since the prospect of trade with the Communist bloc — the Soviet Union, Eastern Europe and China — was heavily restricted through most of the post war period, the influence of this group was necessary, and important in the shift of policy which led to the first sales to the Soviet Union in 1972.[9]

The advocates of commercial trade expansion have been prominent too in supporting a strong US position in response to protectionist measures of any sort by countries which could provide commercial markets, in particular the countries of the European Community.

Others, usually more distant from the farm industry, saw the solution to the burden of price supports in a cut in production, either by taking land out of production altogether or by establishing limits to the amount of price support over and above a certain fixed level. Increasing budget deficits in the 1970s and early 1980s have added to the strength of such arguments.

In 1973, in very tight market conditions, it was economic and consumer interests which dominated the policy-making process. Soyabean export sales were temporarily suspended, despite protests from both producers and those concerned at the longer-term effect on relations with trading partners such as Japan — an importer of soyabeans dependent on US supplies. Fears of shortage and soaring prices within the United States led to Richard Nixon's decision. Though the drama has not been repeated, such purely domestic economic considerations are recognised as part of the decision-making process, particularly by countries heavily dependent on the US for secure supplies.

Ideology too has played its part. The comments by the Agriculture Secretary, Earl Butz, at the end of 1972 which referred to 'getting the government out of agriculture' reflected not just the immediate optimism about world markets after the large Soviet purchases but also a strongly held conviction, traceable from the 1969 inauguration onwards, that free and open markets rather than any price support system represented the most efficient means of supporting US agriculture. The theory was strictly outward-looking, in the sense that it did not incorporate any liberalisation of US import restrictions in the food sector which, particularly in the case of meat production, were and are significant handicaps to other potential producers.[10]

Though never pinned down in a clear government statement, there was also an underlying belief in the words of Emma Rothschild that 'the US should retreat from the arduous costs of world power in economic policy as well as in foreign policies generally'.[11] Butz summarised the position with brevity, 'as we are not the world's policeman, neither are we the world's father provider.'

Butz's statement was offhand and was not endorsed by either the President or by the Secretary of State, Henry Kissinger, who saw a more complex and political role for food exports than either 'aid' or 'trade' alone could offer. The statement did, however, reflect the new definition of American economic interests which evolved in the 1970s. Through each of the Administrations since then it is clear that America's own economic problems and interests at a national level have dominated agricultural trade policy-making.

While balance of payments concerns have encouraged continued government support for agricultural production, with price support necessitated by weak market conditions, grain sales have become much more predominantly commercial. The decline in importance of grain sales under food aid programmes both as a percentage of total grain sales and in absolute terms is indicative of the trend and the extent to which the rhetoric of 'food for peace' heard so often in the 1950s and 1960s has become unfashionable.

Thus macroeconomic considerations, often producing widely varying and inconsistent effects on policy have set the context for decision-making in relation to the farm sector. Congressional votes and indeed the electoral actions of the rural community have provided constraints and parameters within which the policy has evolved, but farm interests are no longer the active driving force they once were.

Within the farming sector itself the development of specialisation in production has altered and weakened the influence of the farm lobby. As producers of a single crop or commodity, farmers no longer adhere to a single set of interests which a general farmers' body can promote. The level of grain prices desired by livestock producers is very different from that sought by the grain farmer. In the words of Lauren Soth:

> General farm organisations such as the Farm Bureau and the Farmers Union have been surpassed in positive promotional power by such groups as the US Feed Grains Council, the National Association of Wheat Growers, the National Corn Growers Association, the National Pork Producers Council and the National Milk Association.
>
> It is certainly arguable that by the mid-1960s the grain trade lobby — the well-organised Washington grouping associated with the major grain trading companies — including Cargill and Continental Grain were more influential in shaping policy than any group of farmers.[12]

What is clear in looking back is that there has been no consistent US agricultural policy — as for instance in the EEC — and that the focus of attention has been the immediate problem rather than the long term. Policy, as the record from PL 480 to PIK shows, has been responsive and no more. At different times one or more of the macroeconomic factors, conditions in particular markets, or specific political considerations have forced the Administration into decisions with consequences beyond the short term. US agricultural policy has become an accumulation of such decisions, and there is no sign yet of any clearer or longer-term strategy.

Grain and Foreign Policy

In addition to domestic policy concerns and macroeconomic issues, agricultural policy has also become the subject of foreign policy considerations as grain exports became not just the source of an important share of farm income but a major factor in world markets.

The potential value of grain exports as a tool in foreign policy was first recognised in the 1950s. The need to clear surpluses from the market combined with the desire to confirm America's relations with emerging Third World countries produced the Agricultural Trade Development Act of 1954, the food assistance programme which was known as PL 480 and was the result of 'an ingenious mixture of altruism, anti-communism and a well-organised commercial lobby'.[13] The stated aim of the law was:

> to develop and expand markets for United States agricultural commodities; to use the abundant agricultural productivity of the United States to combat hunger and malnutrition and to encourage economic development in the developing countries with particular emphasis on assistance to those countries that are determined to improve agricultural production.

The political role of grain supply was always a secondary consideration in the PL 480 programme, as was the altruism. The commercial strategy — of creating with concessionary supplies a series of new markets for future commercial trade — was always the primary factor. It has proved dramatically successful. In South Korea, recipient of much PL 480 assistance during the 1950s and 1960s, trade has now reached the level of over two million tons per year. The pattern of concessionary sales leading to a commercial relationship as development provided the funds to finance imports has been repeated in Taiwan which now buys some $3\frac{1}{2}$ million tons of American grain every year.

Under Title 2 of the original PL 480 law, and the subsequent updating provisions, grain has been used to secure US influence and to assist friendly governments whose survival is seen as a matter of strategic interest by Washington. Some would trace such an approach back to the concessionary supplies provided to Western Europe in the immediate post-war years. The most recent examples are to be found in South Viet Nam, which received $1.3 billion worth between 1965 and 1974, and Egypt which has regularly received as much as 20 per cent of its total grain needs from concessionary US supplies. That flow began after the break in Soviet-Egyptian relations in the early 1970s, and helped to sustain the regime of President Sadat after the riots over food shortages in 1974.

Such assistance marked the incorporation of grain into the general US policy of assisting its allies by economic means. It can barely be described as the use of grain as a weapon or even a bargaining counter.

That very different strategy was born out of the apparent power gained by the United States in the disrupted circumstances of the early 1970s. With shortfalls in harvests and in the supplies of other potential substitutes, the US with its inbuilt surplus dominated the world market. American decisions on sales, whether commercial or concessional, were of critical importance to all importing countries, including of course the Soviet Union.

To Washington, shaken by the oil crisis and the weakness of the dollar, US domination of world trade in grains in the early 1970s offered the chance to use food as a weapon and a sanction against hostile but dependent regimes. The debate on the viability of the food weapon began with the large grain sales to the Soviet Union in 1972. The United States had previously placed embargoes on sales to both Cuba and North Korea but the quantities involved were so small that both countries, with Comecon assistance, could easily find supplies on world markets. The needs of the Soviet Union were different in scale and provoked the demand from those who sought to bolster flagging American leverage in the detente process that US sales of grain be regarded as a reward for particular action — to be withdrawn in times of conflict and disagreement. Kissinger initiated a State Department study of the implications of food power, still unpublished, which according to the Department 'describes the vulnerabilities of certain countries to food embargoes'.[14]

In 1974, responding as much to the need to deal with OPEC as with the implications for detente, the CIA produced a report which concluded that in particular circumstances food power might allow the US 'to regain the primacy in world affairs it held in the immediate post-World War II era'.[15]

In both academic circles and among the farm organisations the concept of US food power has been treated with scepticism. Emma Rothschild writing in 1976 demonstrated how weak the argument for the denial of US supplies was in practice, and concluded that nothing was 'more likely to destroy the influence the United States might have over food importing countries than the possibility of future coercion'.[16] Robert Paarlberg in a series of articles has undermined the credibility of attempts to change Soviet policy in particular by the denial of supplies.[17] The farm lobby, though no keener to see Soviet forces in Afghanistan or Poland than the Carter or Reagan Administrations, has viewed with dismay the effect on American credibility as a supplier of the embargo on sales to the Soviet Union above the 6 million metric tons limit specified by the 1975 Grain Agreement, which the Carter Administration imposed and which ran for 18 months from January 1980.

Events have borne out the case. The Soviet farm sector did

not collapse in the face of the embargo, and the inconvenience was much reduced by the ability and the apparent willingness of the US grain companies to trade with the Soviet Union through European and other non-US agents and ports.[18] In addition, the willingness of the European Community to take up the additional market instead of supporting the embargo seriously undermined its effectiveness.

The response to the embargo was not a military withdrawal from Afghanistan but rather a determination to rebuild Soviet self-sufficiency over a period of years and in the meantime to diversify sources of supply. The US share of the Soviet market thus fell from 75 per cent in 1977 to only 20 per cent, or something over 6 million tons, in 1982/3.

Events have served to prove not only the limitations of the concept of grain power, but indeed the extent of US dependence on secure foreign markets — regardless of their political colour or the activities of their governments. Although some future use of the grain weapon cannot be ruled out, it does appear for the moment that economic considerations are once again the central motivating force of agricultural policy. Given the share of US production going to the world market, those considerations are far from simply domestic in nature. Grain may no longer be regarded as a foreign policy tool, but it is certainly now a foreign policy problem.

The Future Prospects

There are a few fixed and rather more uncertain elements in any calculation of the future prospects of the US agricultural sector.

On the production side a combination of factors suggests continuing growth of potential output — a potential which will be realised unless government acts to restrain it.

Although there is a clear limit to the physical availability of land for production of grain at anything close to today's prices, current usage is well short of that limit.[19] Even discounting the temporary effect of the PIK scheme there is probably as much as 20 per cent more land which could be sown to grain within a single season. The question of yields is less clear, and has been the source of much speculation. Yields have fluctuated but have not in general slowed and the trend is still upwards. As Table 2.9 shows, yields remain well below the yields in a number of other producing regions and

Table 2.9: Comparative Yields (kg/ha)

Total cereals	USA	France	UK	W. Germany	E. Germany	Japan
1974/76	3,339	3,776	3,930	3,973	3,575	5,616
1980	3,774	4,852	4,944	4,429	3,811	4,841
1981	4,278	4,615	4,928	4,450	3,570	5,211
1982	4,409	4,959	5,412	4,858	4,081	5,308
Wheat						
1974/76	1,980	4,078	4,389	4,445	3,949	2,657
1980	2,249	5,169	5,878	4,889	4,384	3,050
1981	2,323	4,809	5,840	5,095	4,358	2,618
1982	2,396	5,232	6,165	5,471	4,986	3,256
Maize						
1974/76	5,165	4,299	2,667	4,995	3,987	2,529
1980	5,711	5,326	785	5,653	4,490	1,989
1981	6,891	5,704	1,000	6,456	4,456	3,000
1982	7,205	6,081	1,000	6,579	4,000	3,000

Source: International Wheat Council, *Annual Statistics*, various issues.

there is some scope for catching up, both between one country and another, and between the average and the best achieved within the US itself.

It would be foolhardy to produce a precise forecast, but it does seem clear that, even discounting major technical breakthroughs in seed development or growing techniques, yields can and will continue upwards, albeit at a modest pace.

The demand side, within the United States, also appears to have its elements of certainty. Total meat demand has barely risen since 1970, responding only in a negative direction to price pressures in the early seventies. The trend from beef to chicken has a generally negative effect on feed grain demand. The poultry industry is more integrated, more mechanised, and significantly more efficient in its use of feed per unit of meat produced. Feed use would clearly decline if the current trend persisted. Population growth, at 0.9 per cent per annum, and growth in per capita income offer the only minor offsetting factors in this situation. Food grain demand has grown similarly slowly, and again seems little affected by rising incomes.

The picture which emerges is of supply continuing to exceed demand by several million tons per annum. If USDA estimates of the growth in stocks (up 12 million metric tons in the one year after the PIK programme) are correct the trend is very significant indeed.

A growing surplus for export would be a welcome prospect for the US government and the nation's farmers if markets for that surplus existed, and if prices were sufficient to cover the costs of production. It is the slippage of those export markets, the loss of a major share of the Soviet trade, and the emergence of well-financed competitors such as the EEC, and relatively low cost producers such as Argentina and Canada, which forced a reluctant Administration into the Payment in Kind programme.

Though feed grain stocks did fall by 75 million metric tons — the cost ($20 billion plus) makes the device uneconomic as a long-term policy option. The Payment in Kind scheme represented a further attempt to extend the practice of voluntary set aside of land in order to achieve a closer balance of supply and demand. The approach of the second Reagan Administration is a very different combination of measures. With a clear long-term commitment to take government out of agriculture, the Administration's 1985 farm bill set support prices at only 75 per cent of the average open market price for the previous five years.[20] David Stockman, then the Administration's Budget Director talked openly of cutting the number of farmers and of treating agriculture as an industry like steel or automobiles — overmanned and in need of rationalisation.[21]

Total farm spending is to be both cut and redeployed with a significant proportion — two billion dollars over three years — devoted to winning back export markets lost to unfair foreign competition — a scarcely veiled code meaning the EEC. The introduction of bonuses, with government-owned surplus stock being provided as a free gift to purchasers of US grain, began with preparations for a sale of 1 million tons of wheat to Algeria in June 1985. In 1979/80, the USA had supplied 41 per cent of the Algerian Market. By 1984/5, aggressive European marketing had reduced the US share to only 16 per cent.

The combination of disengagement from agricultural support and renewed aggression in export policy set the stage for a continuing battle with other agricultural traders. Whether the policy will survive and restore the US trading position or will simply (as suggested by Rob Johnson the Vice President of Cargill[22]) offend existing customers, lower prices and embroil the US in a new form of agricultural support is still a disputed question but given past experience and continuing political pressure to assist the farm states even the US Agriculture Secretary cannot be overly optimistic.

Notes

1. US government statistics, and Lyle Schertz, *Another Revolution in US Farming*, USDA, 1979. A detailed projection of the continuing trend is set out in Farm Credit System's study 'Project 1995'; published in 1985.
2. J.B. Penn in, *Food and Agricultural Policy for the 1980s*, American Enterprise Institute, 1982.
3. Continental Bank Economic Research Division, 1.6.84.
4. D. Gale Johnson in *Food and Agricultural Policy for the 1980s*, AEI, 1982.
5. Jerry Sharples, *An Evaluation of the US Grain Reserve Policy*, Economic Research Service, USDA, 1981.
6. *Financial Times*, 25 August 1983.
7. For a full analysis of the net costs and benefits of the Payment in Kind programme see F. Sanderson, 'A retrospective on PIK', *Food Policy*, May 1984.
8. I. Destler, *Making Foreign Economic Policy*, Brookings, 1980.
9. See Lauren Soth, 'The Grain Export Boom', *Foreign Affairs*, May 1981; Dan Morgan, *Merchants of Grain*, Viking Press, 1979, especially chapter 6.
10. A. Valdes and G. Nores, *Growth Potential of the Beef Sector in Latin America*, IFPRI, 1980.
11. Emma Rothschild, 'Food Politics', *Foreign Affairs*, January 1976.
12. Lauren Soth, 'The Grain Export Boom'. For a full exposition of this view, see Richard Gilmore, *A Poor Harvest — The Clash of Policies and Interests in the Grain Trade*, Longman, 1982.
13. Luther Tweeten, *Foundations of US Farm Policy*, University of Nebraska Press, 1979.
14. *Uses of US Food for Diplomatic Purposes — An Examination of the Issues*, House Committee on International Relations, US Congress, 1977.
15. *Potential Implications of Trends in World Population, Food Production and Climate*, CIA, 1974.
16. Emma Rothschild, 'Food Politics'.
17. Robert Paarlberg, 'Food, Oil and Coercive Resource Power', *International Security*, Fall, 1978; 'Lessons of the Grain Embargo', *Foreign Affairs*, Autumn 1980. *Food Trade and Foreign Policy*, Cornell U.P., 1985.
18. Eric Lindell, 'US Soviet Grain Embargoes. Regulating the MNCs', *Food Policy*, August 1982.
19. Clearly additional land, either of lower quality, or currently used for other purposes such as forestry, would become available over time if its use were made economic by a sustained rise in price. The case against the doomsters who see America running out of land is set out in full in Philip Crowson's *The Cropland Crisis*, Resources for the Future, 1982.
20. *New York Times*, 14 February 1985.
21. *International Herald Tribune*, 14 February 1985.
22. *Financial Times*, 13 June 1985.

3 EUROPE: THE COMMON AGRICULTURAL POLICY AND WORLD MARKETS

Although numerous official and academic studies have been published over the last decade analysing the development and the impact of the Common Agricultural Policy in Europe, few have given more than passing attention to the relationship between agricultural policy within the Community and world market conditions. Countries which earn their livelihoods through the export of agricultural products have long protested about the limitations placed on their potential market in Europe by the mechanisms and workings of the CAP. But only in the last few years as the dynamic effects of generous agricultural support have produced not only self-sufficiency but export surpluses in one commodity after another, has the international dimension of the debate about agriculture in Europe become fully apparent.

Since its inception in the late 1950s, the Common Agricultural Policy has had a dramatic impact on trade flows within the EEC and between the Community and the rest of the world. Table 3.1 demonstrates the progress made towards self-sufficiency in the main cereal crops and animal products since the end of the 1960s. Though still in overall agricultural trade terms a net importer because of large imports of fruit and tropical products which the

Table 3.1: EEC Degree of Self-sufficiency

	1968/70 average	1972/74 average	1978/80 average	1982/84 average
Wheat	90	104	118	131
Coarse grains	81	83	89	99
Sugar	82	91	124	132[a]
Wine	97	99	105	115[a]
Beef and veal	91	92	102	105
Butter	91	98	118	135
All dairy products	96	103	115	125

Note: a. Figures are for 1981/2 only.
Source: USDA, *Western Europe. Outlook & Situation Report*, 1985; EEC Commission, *The Agricultural Situation in the Community*, annual, various issues.

Community at present produces in only minimal quantities, the EEC has emerged over the last two years as a net exporter of beef, for the first time, and as an exporter of wheat on a significant scale. Over the period 1973–80, while imports of agricultural products rose by 83 per cent, exports on a comparable basis rose by 122 per cent and the Community as a whole accounted for almost 15 per cent less of total world trade.

In less than a decade the EEC has established itself as a regular exporter of a number of commodities, taking as much as 12 per cent of the world cereal market in the 1984/5 crop year. Agricultural exports now account for almost 30 per cent of all exports from the Community, against only 9 per cent in 1973.

These figures stand in sharp contrast to the situation twenty years ago when the Community (then of six) was, as a single unit, a significant importer of almost all food products, and a relatively secure market for other agricultural exporters. As recently as ten years ago, the Community was annually importing a net total of 20–30 million tons of grain.

There are three key elements of the CAP which determine and have determined the shifting trade picture. The objective of security of supply contained within the terms of the Treaty of Rome has been interpreted to mean the security achieved through indigenous production, even though the goal of self-sufficiency is not itself explicitly mentioned in any of the clauses setting out the purposes of the CAP. Security has been taken to mean the elimination of avoidable dependence on external suppliers. Though, as the House of Lords Select Committee on the European Communities has pointed out, the degree of dependence on imported fuel and feedstock reduces the strength of the claim to be self-sufficient, on a narrow definition product by product reliance on imports has dramatically declined.[1]

Price guarantees, by providing an assured revenue for all production to all producers, have encouraged and sustained output without the constraint usually provided by price competition.

In the words of the Commission:

As a result of the common Agricultural Policy the Community's degree of self-sufficiency for many of the principal agricultural products has increased. However this development has been accompanied by its own problems due to the fact that the CAP is essentially based on regulatory mechanisms supporting farmers' incomes by means of guaranteed prices or direct product subsidies for unlimited quantities not necessarily geared to the needs of the market.[2]

The pricing mechanism is complex, and should be explained in some detail as its implications dominate the market situation which now exists. A recent study by the International Food Policy Research Institute provides a concise summary:

> The European Community grain economy is largely determined by the Common Grain Market Regulation that came into force on July 1st, 1967. This regulation almost completely disconnected the EEC grain economy from the world market for grain. Domestic grain prices are allowed to vary between the target price and the intervention price. Target prices indicate the prices authorities would like to see prevail on the market, but they imply no direct commitment to enforce those preferences by domestic intervention. Intervention prices are minimum wholesale prices and enforced by direct intervention in the market. Target prices can be equivalent to actual market prices only if domestic self sufficiency is less than 100 per cent. If it is less, domestic EC market prices are determined by the offer price of foreign sellers. However, imports are allowed only at threshold prices, which are entry prices set high enough to guarantee target prices in the EC region with the largest grain deficit which is Duisburg, West Germany. The difference between threshold prices and world market prices at the import harbour with the lowest c.i.f. offer prices by third countries is made up by variable levies. Thus, imports can only enter the EC at threshold prices independent of world market prices. For exports the difference between domestic prices and world market prices is compensated for by export restitutions.[3]

These mechanisms, coupled with the explicit commitment of the CAP to improving productivity, have given added incentives to farmers seeking to mechanise, and to introduce new technology and techniques, with the result that yields have shown considerable improvements. Table 3.2 shows the improvement of yields achieved by the EEC and the extent to which this has continued to outstrip average world yields, while Table 3.3 shows the relationship between world and EEC prices levels over the last decade ·and a half.

Price guarantees have kept land in production, and the combination of factors has produced a steady rise in output. The gearing of prices to marginal costs to protect the least efficient farmer has inevitably brought windfall rents to the larger and to the more efficient producers. Production overall has risen in volume terms by some 3 per cent per year on average since 1973. Import levies and export restitutions determine the precise relationship between agriculture in the EEC and the world market. Export restitutions are not a new device, invented to cope with surpluses, but were established at the inception of the CAP to allow Community exporters to compete on world markets. Since then they have grown both in scope and in cost and in 1982 are estimated to have accounted for 46.4 per cent of the Community's agricultural budget expenditure.

The Common Agricultural Policy is characterised by its lack of any trade component. Trade, either in terms of imports or exports, is merely regarded as a residual consequence of the operations of the other elements of the policy. The Commission, and the member states of the Community, with the exception of France, have only

Table 3.2: A Comparison of Yields (kg/ha)

	World yield	EEC yield	EEC as % of world
Wheat			
1974/76	1,684	3,736	221
1980	1,883	4,486	238
1981	1,890	4,284	227
1982	2,009	4,605	229
Maize			
1974/76	2,722	4,820	177
1980	3,093	5,820	188
1981	3,398	6,410	189
1982	3,465	6,440	186
Barley			
1974/76	1,946	3,650	187
1980	2,036	4,260	209
1981	1,918	4,090	213
1982	2,068	4,430	214
Total cereals			
1974/76	1,954	3,754	192
1980	2,158	4,453	206
1981	2,233	4,357	195
1982	2,307	4,658	202

Source: FAO, *Production Yearbook*, 1982.

Table 3.3: World Market and European Community Threshold Prices for Wheat, Barley and Maize, 1968–81

	Wheat			Barley			Maize		
Year	World market price[a]	EC threshold price	Nominal rate of protection	World market price[b]	EC threshold price	Nominal rate of protection	World market price[c]	EC threshold price	Nominal rate of protection
				(US $/metric ton)					
1968	63.10	115.17	0.83	58.4	92.83	0.59	54.7	93.10	0.70
1969	63.40	115.17	0.82	47.8	96.22	1.01	53.8	97.66	0.82
1970	59.76	115.17	0.93	48.1	97.28	1.02	61.5	98.72	0.61
1971	67.36	115.17	0.71	64.2	97.28	0.52	69.0	98.72	0.43
1972	64.79	125.59	0.94	56.6	109.24	0.93	59.2	106.39	0.80
1973	104.37	140.00	0.34	87.9	123.02	0.40	84.5	120.85	0.43
1974	173.23	154.97	−0.11	139.2	137.26	−0.01	138.1	134.68	−0.02
1975	145.92	179.08	0.23	145.1	157.87	0.09	146.5	156.96	0.07
1976	147.84	184.91	0.25	142.4	163.64	0.15	131.8	163.51	0.24
1977	110.19	205.38	0.86	125.8	181.46	0.44	118.4	182.17	0.54
1978	121.27	239.43	0.97	108.3	215.18	0.99	123.0	199.81	0.62
1979	164.90	274.37	0.66	113.0	244.05	1.16	122.6	244.73	1.00
1980	199.15	296.07	0.49	161.3	264.23	0.64	141.6	264.89	0.87
1981	210.63	284.32	0.35	178.6	253.10	0.42	180.8	253.82	0.40

Notes: EC stands for European Community. The EC threshold price is the average threshold price of the year corrected by quality differences, taking into account the coefficients of equivalence applied by the EC. The nominal rate of protection is the difference between the EC threshold price and the world market price divided by the world market price. The following prices are based on the three specific types of grain.
a. c.i.f. Rotterdam, Red Winter. b. c.i.f. Rotterdam, USA III. c. c.i.f. Rotterdam, USA Corn III.

Source: Commission of the European Community. The Agricultural Situation in the Community, (various issues Brussels: Commission of the European Community, various years).

recently begun to think in terms of an explicit trade policy, defined particularly by the French as a policy for the promotion of exports. To date, in the negotiations of international agreements, and in general trade talks, the motivating force behind the Community's stance has been the protection and the strengthening of its own producers. Trade is regarded as a means of stabilising the internal market, and in John Biffen's words, 'Whereas EEC trade policy as a whole is founded on the principle that the interests of the world community are best served by an open trading system, agriculture is treated separately and stands aside from the rigour of that philosophy'.[4]

In considering the EEC's agricultural trade policy it is important to recognise that the CAP, and the agricultural sector in the Community, are not single entities, and that consideration of aggregate Community trends alone would present an incomplete picture. Agriculture holds a very different status in each of the national economies of the ten member states, with different patterns of production and industrial composition. The institutional structure of the CAP is such that each of the member states have been best able to pursue their own interests, particularly the interests of their farm sectors, by conceding price increases for other products, and other producers, in return for price increases for their own output.[5] This bargaining process between producers in which the consumer is essentially unrepresented has generated a further impetus through the price mechanism to increasing output.

The operation of the budget mechanism is such that each country has a direct incentive to increase its agricultural output.

In each of the member states there has been a trend towards self-sufficiency in main products. Germany, therefore, at the outset considered a major net importer of food, and a market for the agricultural product of the rest of the Community, particularly France, has become a significant producer, approaching self-sufficiency in a number of main crops and is an exporter of wheat. In crops where incentives to production have been highest, output has increased dramatically displacing in the process less well rewarded crops.

Since the institution of the CAP West German agricultural exports have grown at more than twelve times the rate of imports, and in recent years German exports have been rising much more rapidly than French. Germany is now the supplier of over 10 per cent of the wheat traded in the Community. Yet the German farm industry, with over 60 per cent of farmers working in their spare time or on a part-time basis (i.e., with another source of income outside agriculture), is very different from the French. Agriculture in France remains strongly labour-intensive with considerable scope for technological improvements and much larger output expansion. France has long been an exporter of a significant proportion of its farm output. The value of the principle of Community preference, written in at the inception of the CAP for the benefit of the French, has however declined as other member states have improved their own levels of national self-sufficiency. The prospect of a further enlargement of the Community too, with the consequential Spanish challenge to French fruit and wine markets, is not altogether welcome and helps to explain the concentration of current French agricultural policy on the development of Community export policies. The Community's agricultural policy is a key element in domestic French politics, and exports, whether to the other members of the Community or not, are of significant importance to the French balance of payments. In the words of former President Giscard D'Estaing, agricultural trade is for France 'le pétrole vert'.

As Table 3.4 shows, French exports of both wheat and other grains dominate the net trade figures, outweighing the net import positions of the other EEC member states.

The United Kingdom, traditionally a large-scale importer of food from the world market, is gradually finding the pressures and incentives of the CAP a force for change along the German path. Table 3.5 shows the trend in terms of self-sufficiency for cereals and other agricultural products since Britain joined the Community.

UK producers whose efficiency was established under the pre-Community system of agricultural support have been quick to take up the potential increase in output and income. According to the Ministry of Agriculture since the early 1970s the average yields of wheat and barley have risen by 43 and 25 per cent respectively. For the first time since the repeal of the Corn Laws in the 1840s Britain was in 1982 a net exporter of grain.

The Common Agricultural Policy, by inducing increased production across the Community, has reduced the potential for intra-Community trade and has made those countries with particular surpluses look to export markets as a means of disposing of their continuing excess output in the absence of any clear, politically acceptable policy for restructuring the industry.

Table 3.4: Value of Net Cereal Trade: France and the EEC

US $ million	France	Total EEC
Wheat		
1981	2,545.9	1,953.7
1982	1,816.6	1,451.5
1983	2,113.9	1,652.7
Feed grains		
1981	1,343.9	−563.4
1982	1,127.3	−636.6
1983	1,375.9	−330.1
Total including rice and other grains		
1981	4,010.0	2,126.9
1982	2,994.6	1,521.1
1983	3,542.8	2,053.7

Source: USDA Economic Research Service, *Western Europe Outlook and Situation Report*, May 1985

Table 3.5: The Trend in UK Self-sufficiency

	Average 1973/5	1978	1979	1980	1981	1982	1983	1984
Wheat	53	71	75	88	98	108	101	108
Barley	94	121	106	116	141	127	132	151
Total cereals	65	80	71	88	103	105	103	114
Sugar	36	40	47	47	50	57	52	57
Butter	20	40	47	57	56	63	65	60
All food consumed	50	53	54	60	62	62	62	62
All indigenous type food consumed	62	67	69	75	76	77	78	82

Source: Ministry of Agriculture, *Annual Review of Agriculture*, 1986, Cmnd. 9708.

There is one further significant reason which coupled with the CAP goes a long way to explaining the trend in European aggregate trade. That is the relative stagnation in overall consumption of food products. While output, particularly of cereals, has continued to rise, consumption of cereals in total has fallen over the last decade, and while consumption of meat has increased, demand for beef, veal and sugar has grown only marginally.

Three factors can be traced to account for this trend. First, population growth in Western Europe is now slower than in any other region of the world at only 0.2 per cent per annum. The impetus to demand which causes major problems for the developing countries is absent.

Secondly, economic growth has slowed, though this is of relatively minor significance given the fact that consumer spending has continued to increase at a faster rate than the increase in food consumption. Food prices alone cannot be blamed for the level of demand, since in recent years agricultural price increases in the Community have on average been below the rate of inflation, and since the percentage of consumer spending devoted to food has continued to decline.

Substantial food price reductions to the consumer, for instance the cut in British butter prices after the introduction of a special subsidy in the mid-1970s, do not always generate increases in demand.[6]

The third and probably the most important factor is the saturation of demand as socially adequate, as well as nutritionally sufficient, levels of consumption of food products have been reached. The plateauing of food demand suggests that demand patterns will change as a result of changes in consumer preferences and relative prices rather than as a result of any further rises in disposable income.

Consequences for the World Market

The net result of low demand growth, and rising production, has been a gradual decline in imports and a shift in the composition of the total in favour of these products, in particular substitute animal feeds, which are not subject to the import levies of the Community.

Table 3.6 shows the trend. While American supplies of soyabeans under this heading have compensated for the loss of previous and potential grain markets, other producers have found their market share squeezed, and now, with the Community emerging as an exporter, face the prospect of also losing third markets to subsidised European exports. The CAP has as a result had a number of effects on the pattern and structure of the world market.

Efforts to achieve price stability within the Community, and security of supply through import levies and enhanced production, have had the effect of passing the bulk of any instability within the

Table 3.6: Imports of Selected Cereal Substitutes into the European Community, by Country of Origin, 1973–81

Substitute/ Country	1973	1974	1975	1976	1977	1978	1979	1980	1981
Tapioca	1,433	2,073	2,222	2,984	3,801	5,976	5,375	4,866	6,594
Thailand	1,281	1,739	1,873	1,768	3,639	5,668	4,529	4,116	
Indonesia	87	260	314	179	144	219	694	372	
China, People's Republic of	0	4	4	7	1	1	51	336	
Corn gluten feed	837	894	950	1,147	1,405	1,685	2,021	2,596	2,830
United States	754	619	851	1,052	1,363	1,567	1,916	2,476	
Soybean Meal	2,888	3,264	3,321	4,240	4,130	5,918	6,153	7,175	
United States	2,160	2,498	2,013	2,268	1,543	2,674	2,610	3,618	
Brazil	658	666	1,149	1,702	2,225	2,768	3,155	3,226	

Source: European Community, *Analytical Tables of Foreign Trade*, vol. A (Luxembourg Statistical Office of the European Communities various years), chapters 1–24.

Community on to the world market as well as of insulating the Community from world market pressures. The EEC has imported or exported according to its immediate needs and, since the system of controls prevents external circumstances influencing either prices or production levels in the Community, the world market — a relatively small volume of supply compared to total world output and consumption — has been forced to absorb fluctuations. The Community is of course not unique in regarding the world market as a residual supplier or absorber of fluctuations in the domestic market but the scale of EEC output and requirements in relation to world trade enhances its significance:

> The system of variable levies has the effect of increasing world price instability by keeping the Community import process constant and preventing any reaction, either on the supply or the demand side within the Community even to significant changes in world market conditions. Fluctuations therefore have to be absorbed by the world market, which given the slowness of response from either supply or demand, means in effect prices. The most serious impact in conditions of significant shortage and rising prices is therefore likely to fall on importing countries whose stocks are limited. The developing countries among them are likely to suffer doubly if food aid commitments are simultaneously reduced, as was the case in the mid 70s.[7]

Subsidised exports, whether commercial or in the form of food aid, have had the effect of weakening the world market. As Tim Josling has argued, there have been both gainers and losers in the process:

> If, as has undoubtedly been the case developed country farm policies tend to depress world prices for the major temperate zone products in years when supplies are adequate, then developing country importers of these commodities will benefit from substantial improvement in their terms of trade. Since these countries are both more numerous, and more populous than developing country exporters of the same products it is tempting to define such an impact as being in the general interest. The longer term consequences though of the lack of indigenous Third World agricultural expansion must be taken into account.[8]

The net effect of the CAP, by generating relatively cheap supplies for the world market, and by reducing prices, has been to discourage production elsewhere. Exporters in particular are discouraged by the combination of subsidies and the EEC's significant marketing strength. This adds to the disadvantages of developing country producers who seek to penetrate the EEC market itself, and who are confronted not with a quota system but with the use of the price mechanism. The nearest approach to a quota system has been in the sugar market. There the Community has been prepared to guarantee purchases of sugar from the ACP countries (a group of developing countries with special trade arrangements with the EEC), but:

> in practice the politically difficult decision to rein in sugar beet production has been avoided in favour of substantial export subsidies to dispose of surpluses. As a consequence, world free market sugar prices have been depressed. A favoured group of nations sell a sizeable part of their sugar output to the EEC at a high and stable price while the Community still protects its own producers and its processing industry.[9]

While the CAP, through protecting agriculture within the EEC and subsidising exports, clearly distorts the world market and represents a less than optimal allocation, it is possible to define both net beneficiaries and net losers within the overall picture.[10]

Subsidised exports represent on balance a net transfer of resources to developing countries, though only accidentally, and then in a far from optimal manner. Food aid recipients have clearly benefited though food aid is unreliable and reflects the Community's wish to dispose of its surpluses rather than any objective assessment of need or long-term policy. Recipients of the heavily subsidised exports of Community surpluses, such as consumers of butter in the Soviet Union, have also benefited, though not on any regular basis. The most consistent loss has been felt by those exporters of agricultural products who have lost their markets in the EEC and now see their markets in Third World countries threatened by European exports. Australia and one or two South American countries are the most obvious members of this category. For some the operation of the CAP has created new markets. Grain substitute suppliers, particularly Thailand, have benefited from the high prices of European grain and the inducements to beef production which have combined to create a valuable, if somewhat insecure, market for manioc and other substitute feeds which can replace European grown grain. The United States, having lost a significant proportion of its grain market in the Community have found a compensating trade in soyabeans and other substitutes which has sustained a continuing increase in the volume and value of Atlantic trade.

These gains and losses have been at the root of the tension in relations between the European Community and other trading nations over the nature and future of the CAP. The dispute with the United States over agricultural protection has persisted through two decades in a series of disagreements and threats and a general atmosphere of acrimony. Though the wider common interests of the two sides have set limits to the conflict, the dispute has done nothing to improve transatlantic relations. The nature of the dispute has changed gradually as conflicts over access to third markets have been added to the long-standing conflict over American access to the EEC market itself. The increased reliance of the United States farm sector on exports, has sharpened American criticism of the operation of the CAP. The evolution of the dispute is discussed in detail in chapter 7.

The CAP has been the source of conflict with other agricultural producers as well. Australian antagonism to the Community, which goes far beyond resentment at the loss of its traditional British market, reflects the squeezing of Australian trade with the whole of Europe over the last decade, the threat to trade in third markets and the response to the various proposals for extending the CAP, such as the sheepmeat regime. Relations between Australia and the Community countries, collectively and individually, have worsened and Australia has become the most forceful critic of the CAP as an institution, arguing that a continuation of present policies, or their extension, would damage political as well as economic links. In 1980 Australia is reported to have threatened to cancel purchases of the European Airbus to forestall protectionist proposals on sheepmeat, and the questions of uranium supply and Australia's ability to pay for her own defence if agricultural export earnings fell have also been raised.[11] In contrast to the USA, Australia has suffered a major decline in the value of its exports to the Community, not least because of the loss of its quota under the Commonwealth Sugar Agreement.

The criticism of subsidised exports is less than totally justified given the proliferation of export subsidy schemes in all such countries, but the threat posed by the extension of the CAP, and the possible development of an aggressive export policy is now provoking sustained political hostility.

By becoming a force in world markets, reducing prices and threatening market shares, the CAP has created political problems for the Community's external relations, provoking regular references to GATT, and the threat of retaliation as other countries seek to bargain by establishing some form of linkage with other trade issues. The Community has not responded to these problems, and the likelihood must be that they will remain and grow more serious in the immediate future.

The Community's response to the various proposals for trade regulation and liberalisation over the last decade has been essentially concerned with the protection of the farm sector within Europe. Although agricultural goods have been included in many of the Community's international trade agreements, including GATT and the Lomé Convention, the Community has made few significant concessions on the main temperate zone products including grain which form the basis of EEC agriculture.

GATT has been the focus for sharp criticism of the Community with complaints, particularly in relation to the marketing of beef and sugar, on the grounds that export restitutions were giving the Community an inequitable share of work markets. GATT regulations, however, have had little impact on EEC policy. During the establishment of the CAP minor concessions were granted under pressure from the United States to make the Policy compatible with the general principles of GATT. Since then, however, the Community has claimed that the CAP constituted an internal policy, beyond GATT jurisdiction. The Tokyo Round of trade negotiations included an unspecific EEC commitment not to extend its export markets by subsidy, and though this prevented a full-scale challenge to the CAP at the time it was sufficiently vague to permit the debate on a formal, and expansionary, export policy to continue. Over the last two decades the Community has absorbed GATT criticism of the CAP but has rarely responded by changing its policies. Over the period the EEC has probably been more responsible than any other country for the failure of GATT to make any significant progress in liberalising agricultural trade.

The Community has remained unenthusiastic about international commodity agreements affecting its own production, buffer stocks, and attempts to establish a world food regime. In the words of the Overseas Development Institute:

> The Community supports ICAs for those products of which it is an importer (e.g. coffee, cocoa, and rubber) but has difficulty with ICAs for products where it is an exporter. The International Sugar Agreement remains unratified by the Community in view of its unwillingness to accept an export quota.[12]

There has, however, been a significant degree of support from the Community for bilateral deals on agricultural trade. The special status accorded to a limited number of sugar producers, noted above, is illustrative of the attitude. The Lomé Convention and the various Mediterranean agreements have given privileged access to the Community for particular producers, whose output does not threaten European production itself. None of the agreements imply any commitment to production ceilings or limitations.

There is evidence that the pursuit of bilateral arrangements, and negotiations with particular countries and groups of countries with particular common interests, is still the preferred approach to the international market. The Commission's report on the mandate of 30 May 1980 published in June 1981 refers explicitly to 'better organised world markets' and 'cooperation agreements with other major exporters'[13] and it is clear that those who now favour the development of an explicit EEC export policy would wish to use such agreements to control either prices or market shares to the advantage of those producers involved.

It is on the question of market shares that negotiations with other producers are likely to founder as the Community would by implication be committed to increasing its role in world markets by the adoption of an export policy. Agreement on prices, and 'an ordered world market' might be hampered by the relationship between price and market share. The aspiration of the Commission, set out in its report on the mandate of 30 May 'to narrow the gap between levels of institutional support prices and prices ruling on a better organised world market' seems unlikely to be achieved by this sort of agreement. The report implied that an export policy would rely on export credits and long-term supply contracts,[14] both of which would suggest an increased financial commitment, adding to the CAP and the budget cost.

The strong French advocacy of an aggressive export policy is being met by British and West German criticism of the institutionalisation of surpluses, though some commentators have suggested that such a policy might be accepted in the end as part of a new long-term budget settlement in which more of the financial burden of the Community fell on the French.

Many of the advocates of increasing EEC exports rest their case on the view that production costs — particularly the cost of energy, and available land in the United States — will rise, and that world demand, from the Third World, the Soviet Union, Eastern Europe and China, will continue to grow. Deregulation of US energy prices coupled with increasing costs of finding new sources of energy supply will have an effect on agricultural input costs as will any general rise in land values. It is difficult, though, to see these increases forcing US costs up to European levels. Any further general round of energy price rises would in any case affect producers within the Community as well, particularly since the EEC remains significantly less self-sufficient in energy than the United States.

On the demand side the problem is not one of a deficiency of potential demand, whether in Eastern Europe or in the developing countries, but of creating sufficient purchasing power to realise that demand. The Community could conceivably find itself producing surpluses for a commercial market which was growing only slowly, with the only major potential for growth concentrated in the supply of food aid at artificially low or negligible prices. In such circumstances the burden would continue to fall on the EEC's budget.

Despite the hopes of many, both inside and beyond the Community, the pressures for drastic reform of the Common Agricultural Policy appear for the moment at least to have failed.[15]

Although the details remain the subject of intra-Community haggling the CAP as it has evolved over the last two decades appears to have been confirmed by the decisions of successive summits in 1984 and 1985 which accepted that the solution to the Community's budgetary problems lay in an increase in the level of resources provided by the member states. The alternative approach, to treat the resource limit set by the national VAT contributions of 1 per cent as fixed would inevitably have involved the setting of limits on all aspects of farm spending, and probably on the physical volume of farm output as well. Such a limitation might not have ended the problem of surpluses (farm spending might for instance have been partially renationalised, leaving individual governments to sustain output and income levels) but it would almost certainly have brought to an end the current system of universal support for all production, and the allied-system of export restitutions.

The decision to increase Community resources by lifting the ceiling on VAT contributions to 1.4 per cent, first made publicly by the summit of European leaders held in March 1984 under the French presidency offered no such hope of drastic change. Although associated with the simultaneous decision by agriculture ministers to set a physical production limit, with individual quotas, for milk output, the increase in total resources is not tied to any percentage or fundamental change in the operation of the agricultural policy. There will be no fixed limit on total agricultural spending and no automatic quotas or sharp price falls in the support levels for any of the products other than milk which are currently in surplus. Prices will continue to be the subject of year to year intra-Community bargaining.

The coming months will certainly be difficult ones for the Community given the fact that the increased resources will not become available until the decision has been ratified by the parliaments of all the member states. In the grain market in particular, however, the Community may find some respite from its problems and from the cost of export restitutions as a consequence if the weakness of the European currencies against the dollar persists.

This, coupled with the possibility that the Community will seek a further solution to its problems in the establishment of an import levy on cereal substitutes or a volume restriction above which substitutes would be subject to prohibitive duties, would do nothing to ease the tension of trading relations between the Community and the USA.

The introduction of restrictions on cereal substitute trade would run contrary to agreements between the USA, the EEC and other traders reached in the 1950s to leave such products duty free but would reflect the concern felt by the French in particular that the very rapid growth of imports is destroying the demand for indigenous grain. The judgement to be made by the Community will be whether the benefits from reduced export restitution costs in particular would be outweighed by any retaliation, affecting other agricultural products or trade more generally which might be forthcoming from Washington.

Given the apparent strength of commitment to the CAP evidenced by the decisions taken during 1984 such a policy — confirming the existing structure of agriculture and accepting the permanence of existing or still higher levels of production within the Community — could become unavoidable and a permanent, rather than a temporary feature of EEC trade strategy.

The increase in Community resources would, other things being equal, certainly allow the Community to return, in the words of one cynic, to business as usual as regards agricultural support. The vocal protests of French and other farmers suggest that there will be a significant lobby for the cuts in price levels (and thus in many cases the cuts in incomes) made in the past two years to be restored once the new resources are available. However, other things are not likely to be equal and in one respect at least the Community will in 1986 or soon thereafter be facing a new issue which might make even the new spending limits look inadequate. That is the enlargement of the Community to include Spain and Portugal, agreed by the Community in March 1985.

On a static analysis, taking simply the figures of a single year, the effect of Spanish and Portuguese entry could be calculated, and accommodated. Spain and Portugal would absorb a proportion of the Community's current cereal surplus, but would add to the production of fruit, olive oil and vegetables and to the existing wine surplus. The deficit of the two countries in the cereal market could reduce substantially if not totally the cost of export restitutions for cereals, currently running at some £700 million per year though at the cost of forcing American exports to Spain out of the market. US grain exports to Spain have already fallen as a result of the increase in Spanish feed grain production from 11.6 to 19.5 million metric tons between 1981 and 1984. High support prices and preparations for accession are already having their effect.

But the relief might only be of short-term value, and it is in the dynamic, rather than the static situation created by accession that the real problems have been identified.

In part, any analysis depends upon the extent to which the Community supports the production of wine, olive oil and other Mediterranean products where substantial surpluses are in prospect in a Community of twelve. Beyond that comes the broader question of the development of consumption and production. If Spain and Portugal provide extensive new markets for existing output the saving would be considerable. The strong possibility, however, is that price incentives coupled with structural investments in irrigation and other technical improvements would induce over time a growth in output far beyond the likely consumption increase, thereby adding to the EEC surpluses and costs.

Under present arrangements, the Mediterranean products receive only a fraction of the total amount spent under the terms of the CAP. Only some 4 per cent goes to fruit and vegetable producers, and 2 and 1 per cent respectively to tobacco and wine. Spanish and Portuguese entry will bring into the Community hundreds of thousands of small producers, seeking to improve their present meagre incomes through guaranteed prices, and at the same time carrying with them the potential of modernisation and consequent major increases in output — 77 per cent of Spanish, and 90 per cent of Portuguese farmers work less than 10 hectares.[16]

Spain, with some 15 per cent of its population directly employed in agriculture, and Portugal with 25 per cent, would add two-thirds to the agricultural population of the EEC. The desire for common facilities and support would be strong, while the ability of the Spanish and particularly the Portuguese, with GNP both in absolute and per capita terms well below the EEC average, to contribute through the current financial structure to common funding would be very limited.

The willingness of the two potential new members to accept an unchanged CAP, without any further extension of EEC provisions for Mediterranean producers is made less likely by the fact, noted by John Marsh and other commentators that without change the Mediterranean countries will be major net losers. Both Spain and Portugal would suffer in resource and welfare terms from a system which required them to pay more for their imports (i.e., to pay Community-level, rather than world-level prices). The current bias in the CAP towards the 'Northern European products' such as cereals would result, if it were left unchanged, in both Spain and Portugal emerging as net contributors to the European budget, regardless of their relative poverty.

The process of Spanish and Portuguese integration may be gradual, and spread over a number of years because of the elaborate transition processes within the Treaty of Accession, but the continuing process faces the Community with pressure for decisions on its future scale and shape.

A decision to establish a full-scale regime for Mediterranean products would add to costs, since the Community is already a net exporter of a number of the products concerned and would be a substantial net exporter if Spain and Portugal were taken into account. A new regime designed to assist Spanish producers would cut across existing agreements with the associates of the Community around the Mediterranean whose exports to the EEC would be badly hit by a common EEC policy, and the variable levies, export restitutions and other devices which would accompany it. Other third world country producers would also be adversely affected.

An extension of current common price regimes to the Spanish and Portuguese might well also have the effect of stimulating production to the extent that short-term savings created by current deficiencies would become still greater costs as a result of new surpluses. Spanish agriculture is weak both in technological application and structure but its potential is considerable, as the growth of production since the end of the Franco era has already demonstrated.

Notes

1. House of Lords, Select Committee on the European Communities, *Report on Agricultural Trade Policy*. November 1981.
2. European Commission, *Guidelines for European Agriculture*, Com: 10311/81.
3. Ulrich Koester, *Policy Options for the Grain Economy of the European Community*, International Food Policy Research Institute, 1982.
4. Speech to the Trade Policy Research Centre, London, July 1981.
5. The structure is described in detail in Joan Pearce, *The Common Agricultural Policy, Prospects for Change*, Royal Institute of International Affairs, 1981.
6. *The Future Direction of the CAP*. Paper to the Agricultural Economics Conference, December 1981, by David Williamson, Deputy Director General for Agriculture in the European Community. Williamson draws the conclusion that since both population and demand are static, the Community must place its emphasis for the future on a commercial export policy.
7. S. Tangermann, *Food or Famine*, Gottingen, 1981.
8. T.E. Josling, 'The European Community's Agricultural Policy and the Interests of Developing Countries', *ODI Review*, 1979.
9. Ibid.
10. In his recent study, *Policy Options*, Ulrich Koester estimated the welfare gains of a liberalisation of the Community's grain policy. The figures show clearly that the gains would accrue to the United States, Canada and Australia with almost all the other countries in the world suffering a net loss of welfare as a result of increased prices and reduced food aid availabilities. On the first order effects (i.e., without taking into account the effect on other commodities) Koester estimated a net welfare loss of 0.4 per cent of GNP for the developing countries.
11. Joan Pearce, *The Common Agricultural Policy*.
12. Evidence submitted by the ODI to the House of Lords Select Committee, *Agricultural Trade Policy Report*, page xviii.
13. European Commission Com (81) 300: 8144/81.

14. The Agriculture Committee of the European Parliament in a subsequent report (1 – 30/82B 19 March 1982) explicitly advocated such contracts.

15. For a range of views on the alternative paths of reform see the *European Review of Agricultural Economics*, vol. 11.2, 1984, and in particular Stefan Tangermann, Georges Bublot and Louis Mahé.

16. *The Times*, 17 July 1985.

4 THE SOVIET UNION

The third key actor in the international grain market is the Soviet Union. For decades before the First World War Russia was one of the world's leading exporters of grain, supplying not only parts of Germany and the Austro-Hungarian Empire but also Britain with wheat and other grains. The Russian fleet dominated European trade in grain and access to Russian wheat supplies was an issue of political concern and even of conflict. The 1917 Revolution did not bring an immediate change of circumstances. For several decades grain remained crucial to Soviet trade, earning Western currency and maintaining economic links with the West. The volume of exports did not show any marked increase but the Soviet Union managed, by rationing domestic supplies, to remain a net exporter on a limited scale and as recently as the late 1960s was supplying Eastern Europe and a number of countries beyond Comecon on a regular basis. Grain exports were a source not only of revenue but also, in certain cases, of political influence. The pattern of Soviet exports and their destination is shown in Table 4.1.

In the 1981–2 crop year, by contrast, the Soviet Union imported some 45 million tons of food and feed grains (20 million tons of wheat, and 25 million tons of feed grains), almost a quarter of all internationally traded grain. Over a third came from the United

Table 4.1: Soviet Grain Exports (000 million tons)

Period average To:	1956/60	1961/65	1966/70	1971/75
North Korea	38	98	170	176
Egypt	203	–	359	–
Finland	336	175	34	13
UK	103	306	195	56
Yugoslavia	175	14	–	–
CMEA members	4,122	4,224	4,313	4,326
Total exports	5,906	5,879	5,622	5,732
Total imports	384	3,497	2,866	13,188
Net trade	+5,521	+2,281	+2,755	−7,455

Source: USDA, *USSR Outlook and Situation Report*, various issues.

States. Current estimates of the 1984 crop year suggest that despite initial optimism production was again well below 200 million metric tons and that the volume of imports rose to a record level of more than 57 million metric tons. The evidence is that even at these levels the excess of world supplies is allowing the Soviet Union to pick and choose its trading partners. Nevertheless, it will remain the largest single importer in the world, dependent for over 20 per cent of its total consumption on foreign suppliers. Soviet dependence on foreign grain has not fallen below 30 million tons in any year since 1978.

On two occasions in the last decade the United States has cut off or restricted supplies to the Soviet Union, and in the United States the vulnerability of the USSR to such embargoes and the potential for their future use remain live issues of debate.[1] The economic independence considered vital by the founding fathers of the Soviet state for the survival of communism in Russia has been put in jeopardy by shortages of the most basic commodity.

There are a number of contributory factors which explain the dramatic switch. First and foremost are the limitations of Soviet agriculture. Soviet farmland, though equal in acreage to that of the United States, is of limited quality for intensive production. Much of the Soviet Union is too dry to establish normal production patterns. Rainfall is quite variable, ranging anywhere from 8 to 23 inches a year. Only 1 per cent of Soviet farmland receives 28 inches of rainfall a year, an amount that nearly all American states receive regularly. Another problem is soil conditions. Where rainfall is plentiful the land is covered by coniferous forests and the soil is acidic.

The additions to the cultivated area in the Soviet Union made by successive governments since the 1950s have added land of poorer quality, keeping average yields low, as shown in Table 4.2.

With only a slight reduction in cultivated area, yields appear to have fallen badly in the last two years.

Almost two-thirds of Soviet grain lands are located in areas where precipitation and growing seasons are barely adequate for grain production and therefore a relatively limited change in the climate can reduce crops drastically. Climatic conditions, including the irregularity of rainfall and the destructive drying winds are anything but favourable for a country relying on steady output from these areas.

Table 4.3, showing output of wheat and barley over the last

Table 4.2: USSR Grain Yields (metric tons per hectare)

	Wheat	Barley	Oats	Total grain
1966/70	1.34	1.50	1.38	1.37
1971/5	1.45	1.53	1.31	1.47
1976/80	1.64	1.63	1.42	1.60
1981/4	1.45	1.36	1.29	1.43

Source: USDA, *USSR, Outlook and Situation Report*, 1985

Table 4.3: USSR Grain Output, 1971–81 (million metric tons)

	Wheat	Barley	Total grain
1971	99	34	181
1972	86	37	168
1973	109	55	222
1974	83	54	196
1975	66	36	140
1976	96	69	223
1977	92	52	196
1978	120	62	237
1979	90	48	179
1980	98	43	189
estimates 1981	80	38	160
estimates 1982	85	41	170
estimates 1983	80	54	185
estimates 1984	75	40	160

Sources: USDA, *USSR, Outlook and Situation Report*, various issues, and International Wheat Council Review of the World Wheat Situation 1984/85.

decade, shows just how significant the variations from year to year have been.

Peak output in the excellent conditions of 1978 was 25 per cent above average. Output in 1981, was, according to the best estimates available, only 80 per cent of average. Some sources suggest that 160 million tons may even be an overstatement, speculation fuelled by the Soviet failure to publish its own figures for the year.

Soviet agriculture has also suffered over the years from poor management, and the low priority, in comparison with industry, given to it by central government. Only in recent years, under the pressure of a substantial agricultural trade deficit has sustained central government attention, and more important investment, been focused on the development of the farm sector. Agriculture in the Soviet Union has yet to escape the consequences of the forced disruption of the kulaks' production system by Stalin or to conquer the excessive stifling degree of bureaucracy involved in agricultural decision-making — an involvement made even less productive by the quality of the bureaucrats concerned.

The result of this combination of factors has been that the resources devoted to agriculture have often been under utilised:

> Each year Soviet factories turn out 550,000 tractors but each year almost as many are scrapped after only a short working life. A high percentage of available tractors, combine harvesters and other expensive machines are always out of action because of insufficient quality control, lack of spare parts and servicing facilities.[2]

Infrastructure is often inadequate or non-existent and the co-cordination of farm needs with the provision of secondary inputs, from machinery to fertiliser, is chaotic.

As a result, the efficiency of farming in the Soviet Union has barely improved since the 1960s. Feed conversion ratios for pigs, for instance, remain at twice the level achieved in the West. Soviet figures show consumption of 9.1 units of oats (the standard Soviet feed measure) for every unit of output or gain in live weight in 1979. In the mid-sixties the average was 9.4. Even with a generous adjustment to allow for differences in measurement techniques and grain quality, the figure is still more than double the average West German farm ratio, of 3.5 to 4 kilograms of grain per kilogram of gain in weight.[3] On more general figures, Soviet meat output rose by some 73 per cent between 1961 and 1980. Feed grain use rose from 40 million tons to 126 million tons over the same period, an increase of over 200 per cent. A simple calculation even from these broad figures demonstrates the inefficiency of Soviet farming.

Efficiency is not helped by the absence in the communal sector as organised in the Soviet Union of any incentive (in any form, whether financial or not) for the Soviet farm worker to give attention to the quality of his work and output. In Alec Nove's words:

> The problem is one of labour incentives in the excessively large farms, which often have around 500 members or employees, scattered in several villages and engaged in a multitude of activities cultivating numerous crops and keeping every kind of farm animal. A sort of diseconomy of scale (or alienation if one

prefers the word) then develops. The peasants do not feel responsible for the final outcome and indeed there is often little visible connection between the quality of their work and the harvest. A frequently cited example relates to tractor drivers engaged in ploughing. They are paid on piece rates, measured in terms of hectares ploughed, and receive bonuses for economising on fuel and avoiding breakages. All these indicators 'benefit' from ploughing as shallowly as possible. The resultant losses in the harvest cannot be ascribed to the individuals concerned. So the fact that the tractor drivers are well paid in no way ensures that they perform their work efficiently![4]

The small private sector, though more efficient, has also been unable to respond to the country's needs given the lack of rewards, until the recent increase in procurement prices, and the difficulties associated with the still centrally directed system by which all farm inputs are supplied.

Increases in output have been achieved only by a massive and often apparently haphazard injection of resources. Until recently it appeared that the non-financial problems of the farm sector — management, organisation and structure — were ignored as politically embarrassing.

Given all these limitations and obstacles, it is perhaps legitimate as some commentators have suggested to discuss Soviet agriculture in terms of remarkable progress rather than in terms of relative failure. In terms of calories consumed Soviet averages certainly match the figures for the West, and fall only a little short of US levels. They are well above the levels of either India or China.

The achievements of the distribution system, which now ensures a physiologically adequate diet for all Soviet citizens, deserves full recognition. Annual average grain production has risen from 130 million tons during the 1961–5 plan period, although the first four years of the current five-year plan show a fall of 15 per cent from the 205 million metric tons per annum average between 1976 and 1980.

There are now 115 million head of cattle in the Soviet Union and some 1,000 million poultry against 75 million cattle and 500 million poultry twenty years ago.

Despite these achievements Soviet agriculture has been unable to meet the demands placed upon it. The growth of the Soviet population from 190 million in 1939 to 208 million in 1959 and at a rate of almost 1 per cent per year since then to its present level of 265 million has added inexorably to the country's food needs. In addition, relatively strong growth in the industrial sector and in the economy as a whole has given Soviet workers real increases in income. An improvement in the standard diet, away from the past preponderance of potatoes and starch and in favour of meat was an unavoidable consequence of the economic process but one which could not readily be met by the farm sector. Low consumer prices for food, heavily subsidised by central government and, in the case of bread, held static now for over twenty years, added to demand while doing nothing to encourage production.

The shift in the pattern of trade began in the late 1960s and early 1970s and followed a conscious change of Soviet policy in favour of the consumer. The change can be traced back to the accession of Mr Brezhnev, and the March 1965 plenum of the Communist Party Central Committee, since when there have been large-scale investments in agriculture of resources and technology.[5] 'Sometime in the 1960s the leaders of the Soviet Union decided to increase their people's consumption of meat and dairy products and to keep that increase steady by not slaughtering livestock when harvests failed.'[6] The motivation behind this policy was the sharp rise in disposable incomes which accompanied growth in the Soviet economy, coupled with the realisation that provision of other consumer goods was not one of the success stories of the Soviet state's first half-century. Housing, in particular, was inadequate, but a rapid improvement of housing provision would have meant a diversion of resources including, most importantly, scarce manpower from the industrial sectors of the Soviet economy. The decision to concentrate on increasing meat output and consumption soon began to have its effect: 'Between 1968 and 1971 there was a 40 per cent increase in the use of feed grains in Russia and livestock herds expanded. If there were any doubts, they probably disappeared in 1970 when Polish workers rioted in Gdansk and Szczecin after food shortages and price rises'.[7]

The Soviet farm sector, however, found itself unable to respond to the challenge despite increased investment, increased effort devoted to mechanisation and the elimination of waste and despite the introduction of some limited new methods of farm control and management. Livestock numbers increased, and meat output and consumption stabilised. The grain sector, however, could not meet the targets set for it. The small-scale occasional use of the world market to supplement domestic supplies envisaged by Soviet planners when the programme began has turned into a frequent, almost permanent reliance on imports with the pattern made unpredictable by the periodic failure of the Soviet crop and by climatic conditions. Table 4.4 shows the pattern of Soviet imports over the last decade, leading up to the four consecutive years when harvests fell significantly short of the targets set in the plan, and when imports were at their highest.

The cost has been estimated at $5 billion in 1980 rising to perhaps $7 billion in 1982. The Soviets have been assisted by low and falling real grain prices on the world market but have still found themselves paying out up to a quarter of their hard currency export earnings for grain supplies.

To date the Soviets have persisted with their strategy of maintaining herds through all but the worst shortages even at the cost of large-scale imports though there is evidence that concern over the cost and the degree of external dependence is growing. Recent Soviet statements, including the most recent food programme,[8] suggest that self-reliance in terms of feed production is being reasserted as a medium-term aim and that the Soviet Union has no intention of remaining an importer on the current scale. The programme even talks, somewhat optimistically of 'grain for export', and sets targets for production of 255 million tons per year on average between 1985 and 1990, with a strong bias to feed grain, as well as confirming meat consumption targets of 70kg per capita for the end of the decade. The expectation must be that these

Table 4.4: Soviet Grain Imports: Volume and Value

	Wheat	Coarse grains (million metric tons)	Total	Estimated cost (US$m)
1974/75	2.5	2.7	5.7	758
1975/76	10.1	15.6	26.1	2,766
1976/77	4.6	5.7	11.0	3,056
1977/78	6.6	11.7	18.9	1,474
1978/79	5.1	10.0	15.6	2,483
1979/80	12.0	18.4	31.0	3,598
1980/81	16.0	18.0	34.8	5,187
1981/82	20.0	25.0	45.5	8,366
1982/83	21.0	19.0	40.0	6,720
1983/84	23.0	11.0	34.0	5,362
1984/85	29.0	28.0	57.0	7,100

Source: USDA, *USSR. Situation and Outlook Report*, various issues and the International Wheat Council, *Market Report*, various issues.

objectives will be confirmed by the new leadership under the 12th Five-Year Plan.

Soviet plans, however, are rarely fulfilled in total and it is important to examine one by one the various factors which will determine the equation of demand and supply and thereby establish the requirements from trade.

On the demand side, rising incomes leave the logic which led to the decisions of the early Brezhnev years unchanged: 'According to the official Soviet statistics, total monetary wage income per head of the population had risen by 207 per cent by 1980 as compared to 1960, and the population by 24 per cent. Some put the income elasticity of demand for better food, with meat taking the lead at 0.8 . . . demand for meat must therefore have more than trebled.'[9]

Meat consumption, per capita, has in fact risen by only 40 per cent over the last twenty years. The increases projected for 1990 in the food programme are themselves relatively modest and should be considered in the context of recent reports that the Soviet economy is continuing to expand at 3 or 4 per cent each year.

Tables 4.5 and 4.6 show the relatively favourable performance of the Eastern European members of the Council for Mutual Economic Assistance, a comparison which appears to be prominent in the thinking of Soviet planners and politicians. Even if the target of meat consumption for 1990 set in the food programme is achieved, consumption per head will still be well below the *current* Eastern European average. Fulfilment of the target will not be sufficient to satisfy demand in full. Price increases long resisted by

Table 4.5: Per Capita Meat Consumption, Centrally Planned Economies, 1965–81 and projected 1985 (kilograms)

	1965	1971	1975	1980	1981	1985
Bulgaria	40	44	58	61	63	66
Czechoslovakia	62	74	81	85	85	81
GDR	59	68	78	89	89	86
Hungary	52	60	68	70	70	72
Poland	49	56	70	74	64	66
Romania	23	29	46	60	59	64
Yugoslavia	27	38	48	56	56	58
USSR	41	50	57	57	56	60
China				10		11

Source: G. Vitanova, *Trade Prospects for Centrally Planned Economies*, Agriculture Canada, 1982.

Table 4.6: USSR and Eastern Europe: Average Food Consumption (kg per head)

a. In USSR

	1965	1980[a]	1990 plan
Meat and products	41	58	70
Fish and products	12.6	17.6	19
Milk and products (in terms of milk)	251	314	330–40
Eggs (units)	124	239	260–8
Sugar	34.2	44.4	45.5
Vegetable Oil	7.1	8.8	13.2
Vegetables	72	97	126–35
Potatoes	142	112	110
Fruit and berries	28	38	66–70
Bread products (in terms of flour)	156	139	135

b. In East European Countries[b] in 1980

	Bulgaria	Hungary	GDR	Poland	Czechoslovakia
Meat and products	65.9	70.5	89.4	82.1	85.0
Fish and products	6.6	2.5	7.5	8.1	5.4
Milk and products (in terms of milk)	227	162[c]	na	451	230
Eggs (units)	203	342	290	223	316
Sugar	34.2	35.0	40.7	41.4	38.0
Vegetable oil	15.1	6.0	1.7	2.6	7.3
Vegetables	126	na	96.8	101[d]	68
Potatoes	26.1	62	142	158	75
Bread products (in terms of flour)	160	115	94.2	127	107

Source: Statistical year book of CMEA countries for 1981.
Notes:
a Figures quoted by Brezhnev on 24 May 1982; in some cases these are marginally higher than those reported in the 1980 Soviet statistical handbook.
b Excluding Romania, which does not publish per capita food consumption figures.
c Excludes butter.
d Excludes processed vegetables.

Soviet governments could be used to contain purchases, but there is so much 'pent up demand (cash) in the USSR that price measures would have to be of an extremely drastic kind if they were to have a real effect.'[10]

The conclusion on the demand side is that the Soviet government will stick to its plans for gradually improving meat consumption levels in all circumstances short of a national emergency or war, and will therefore sustain much of the investment anticipated in the food programme.

On the supply side the problems which have long beset the production system remain. The growth of meat imports over the last decade, an almost unnoticed feature of Soviet trade which is set out in Table 4.7, has reflected the poor response to attempts to achieve improvements in the efficiency of the livestock sector.

Recent reports suggest that uncertainty remains over the policy of expanding livestock inventories. A reversal of policy emphasising herd growth as the best way of expanding supplies appears to be taking place. Instead inventories will grow more slowly with the aim of achieving shorter fattening periods and better feed conversion ratios. None but the most optimistic Soviet commentators expect early or spectacular results from this policy.

Land use for grain production has fallen back a little from its peak of 130 million hectares, reflecting the fact that the peak included the use of highly marginal land. Table 4.8 shows the pattern of total land use, and use for each of the various main crops.

There is some evidence that some very poor land is still being farmed, and some land overfarmed. No further major increase of arable land seems possible in the foreseeable future. The addition of newly drained and irrigated land to the stock is barely keeping pace with losses caused by rising salinity, urban growth and mining. Policies for increasing fertiliser use, mechanisation and technological development have been reemphasised and have been given greater priority in closely related industrial plans, and in terms of investment. Overall investment in agriculture will rise from 27 per cent of the national total to 33 per cent by the end of this decade, according to the new programme, though as yet it is far from clear which sector will suffer the compensating reduction. Nor is it clear that Soviet agriculture and industry will respond other than in its past sluggish way to large injections of resources. Although some decentralisation of management and decision-making is promised, the effectiveness of the plan has yet to be seen. The much publicised establishment of a coordinating authority between the various sectors of the industry — from suppliers to marketers at the 'raion', or district level is potentially valuable but could equally become a further layer of bureaucracy in addition to the many which already exist. No proposals to abolish other layers have been made. The raising of procurement prices, earlier in the period of the current plan, may in the end prove a more effective instrument, though the

Table 4.7: Meat Imports: Volume and Value

	Red meat	Poultry (million tons)	Total	Estimated value (US$m) current dollars
1972	40	45	131	96
1973	46	43	129	111
1974	396	76	515	476
1975	406	48	515	495
1976	226	58	362	379
1977	438	121	617	692
1978	84	52	184	258
1979	386	141	611	844
1980	577	159	821	1,359
1981	n.a.	n.a.	980	1,647
1982	n.a.	n.a.	939	1,430
1983	n.a.	n.a.	985	1,370

Source: USDA, USSR. *Outlook and Situation Report*, 1985.

Table 4.8: Land Use (000 hectares)

	Wheat	Rye	Barley	Oats	Grains	Total land use
1966/70 a.v.	67,174	11,505	20,331	8,680	122,038	n.a.
1971/5 a.v.	61,469	8,500	28,370	11,310	123,988	548,812
1976/80 a.v.	60,711	7,714	34,011	12,080	127,905	n.a.
1981	59,232	7,551	31,781	12,470	125,559	553,751
1982	57,278	9,829	29,706	11,489	123,012	556,268
1983	50,823	10,334	31,679	12,389	120,809	n.a.
1984	51,061	9,420	30,426	12,806	119,612	n.a.

Source: USDA, *USSR. Situation and Outlook Report*, various issues.

cost to the Soviet taxpayer, coupled with the cost of heavily subsidised consumer prices, could become a major burden setting a limit to the use of the policy. According to one source the cost of food subsidies in 1980 was probably some $46 billion, a figure which if correct would represent 10 per cent of Soviet government spending.

To meet the demand level set in the food programme, even on the assumption of a positive if modest improvement in the efficiency of animal feed use (i.e., in the output of meat per unit of feed consumed) the output of grain would have to rise by some 70 million tons per annum between now and 1990 from the average figure of the last four years (that average being a more realistic starting point for any calculation than the level set in the current five-year plan). Any additions to that to provide levels of stocks which could sustain the country through crop failure would push the required rate of expansion up to 7 per cent per annum.

Taking the average of one five-year plan period against the next, the Soviet Union has never achieved a rate of expansion faster than 5 per cent per annum, and then only from a much lower base. If this were matched in the next five years or even slightly exceeded it would still leave a shortfall of over 20 million tons (excluding stock change) to be found from imports even in years when climatic conditions were reasonably favourable.

Such a forecast, which if anything errs on the optimistic side from the Soviet point of view, raises a number of questions. The first is the ability of the Soviet Union to fund purchases on a sustained basis at such a level. Recent research has emphasised the vulnerability of the Soviet trade position, and in particular the impact on Soviet fortunes of the oil price.

Between 1978 and 1981 the Soviet import bill for grain rose by 104 per cent from some $2.5 billion to over $8 billion. The 57 million tons imported in 1984/5 would probably have pushed the cost back up to that level but for lower world prices. Over the 1978 to 1980 period the Soviet Union's overall hard currency trade deficit of $3.8 billion was kept at a reasonable level only by revenue raised from energy sales. The additional $11.8 billion earned from energy exports raised total hard currency earnings from $13.2 billion in 1980 concealing a decline in other exports of some $1.1 billion.

The crucial importance of energy sales to the Soviet balance of payments at a time when oil prices have declined sharply and hard currency debts (estimated at $13 to $15 billion) are proving costly to service indicates one of the key constraints on Soviet grain purchases.

The reports that extended credit of up to 180 days is now being sought by the Soviets for up to 75 per cent of their grain imports may be an indication that even in a period when grain prices are low, financial constraints are affecting Soviet strategy.[11]

If balance of payments questions are to be set against the essentially political issue of consumer demand, and the extent to which that demand can be satisfied in determining the level of imports, there will still remain the secondary question as to the source of those imports.

Both the variations in import levels, and the manner in which the

Soviet Union has approached the world market, have tended to be destabilising over the last decade. From the time of the first large-scale imports, the so-called 'great grain robbery of 1972', the Soviets have utilised the advantages of a single trading agency, Exporthleb, which has conducted its operations in almost total secrecy, exploiting the rivalries and competition which exist between the various grain exporting nations and between the grain companies:

> The Soviet Union's procurement practices are identical in many respects to those of the most sophisticated privately owned grain firms. Exporthleb, the official grain trading arm, has free rein to exercise whatever commercial muscle it can to satisfy Soviet import-export requirements . . . It is a tough merchant, using monopoly powers to play off governments and countries against one another.[12]

The Soviet Union appears to have held to the letter of contracts signed at all times, but has always been prepared to make the fullest use of the market system. The record of the last decade clearly shows that 'the Soviet Union is a most capable importer, effectively using its monopoly of factual information concerning its own situation and intentions'.[13]

Long-term supply agreements have come to play an increasingly important part in the Soviet use of the world grain market. Table 4.9 shows the extent of commitments in mid-1984. In addition to those listed, the USSR has agreed in principle to import 400,000 metric tons per annum from Hungary over a three year period, and to boost imports from France by unspecified volumes. The deals with Canada, Argentina and the other suppliers are in addition to the agreements reached with the United States.

The first of these, the 1975 agreement which ran until 1981 and which was extended for two further years, covered sales of wheat and other grain by the USA and set minimum levels of imports by the Soviet Union, at six million tons per annum, and a higher level of 8 million tons above which specific permission from the US government is required for any purchases. The agreement did not succeed in stabilising the trade which has fluctuated erratically. The volume of trade has varied from a high of 23 million metric tons of grain in 1979 to a low of perhaps as little as 7 million metric tons in 1982.

Table 4.9: USSR Import Commitments for Grain under Existing Agreements

Supplying Country	Date announced	Duration years	from	Quantities and specifications
Argentina	July 1980	5	1/7/80	4.5 million metric tons of maize (corn), sorghum and soyabeans annually
Brazil	March 1982	4	1/1/83	0.5 millions metric tons of maize (corn) annually
Canada	May 1981	5	1/8/81	25 million metric tons of grain from August 1981 to July 1986[a]
Hungary		3	1/1/83	At least 0.4 million metric tons of wheat and maize per annum
EEC	October 1982	3	1/1/83	Unspecific agreement to increase volume of French grain exports.
United States	July 1983	5	1/10/83	Minimum 8 million metric tons of grain annually, comprising approximately equal amounts of wheat and maize (corn).

Note: a. No annual minimum specified. Shipments in 1981/82 amounted to 7.8 million metric tons.
Source: International Wheat Council, *Market Report*, September 1984.

Table 4.10: Value of US–Soviet Trade in Grain, 1975–84 (US$ million)

	Wheat	Coarse grains	Total agricultural trade
1975	672.7	457.8	1,170.3
1976	264.2	1,180.2	1,604.8
1977	426.8	412.4	1,052.8
1978	355.8	1,109.4	1,765.1
1979	813.2	1,572.0	3,000.1
1980	336.1	692.9	1,137.8
1981	772.6	801.4	1,684.7
1982	802.2	834.6	1,866.2
1983	800.6	404.4	1,472.9
1984	1,170.8	1,450.4	2,877.1

Source: USDA, *USSR. Situation and Outlook Report*, 1985.

The basic terms of the agreement survived President Carter's embargo in January 1980 but the spirit of economic detente and mutual benefit which lay behind the settlement reached in 1975 have never recovered from the reintroduction by the US administration of a political element into its grain export commitments. Despite President Reagan's repeated offers of large quantities of US grain (well above the levels prescribed in the agreement) in each of the last two crop years, and a proferred guarantee that grain would not be embargoed again except in circumstances of direct conflict, the Soviet Union has continued to seek diversified sources of supply.

Although the 1980 embargo did create inconvenience and some hardship it had only a slight effect on grain availability in the Soviet Union. Supplies were available as a result of the ability of the grain companies to ship supplies through their various national subsidiaries, and the willingness of the EEC to act as an entrepot for supplies from the USA:

> In recent years there has been a dramatic decline in the percentage of grain sales made to the Soviet Union directly through the home offices of US grain multinationals. In 1976/77 65 per cent of the wheat and corn sold to the Soviets by US grain MNCs was through their home offices in the US and the remaining 35 per cent was sold through these subsidiaries. Finally by 1979 American grain MNCs no longer made any Soviet sales through their US offices; all grain sold to the Soviets was through the foreign offices. US grain MNCs undertook this shift in policy over the course of late 70s for one primary reason — to circumvent US export control regulations.[14]

More important than the inconvenience was the effect on Soviet attitudes to trade with the USA. The embargo was a gesture of protest in which a moral cause superseded any consideration of the USA's short- or medium-term economic interests. The condition of the market, in which prices were low and supplies abundant was ignored, as was the ability of the Soviet Union to meet its needs from elsewhere.

The net effect of the embargo was to damage America's reputation as a source of secure supplies, and, once the restrictions on trade had been lifted, to ensure that the Soviet Union would approach the United States only as a residual supplier. There is no evidence that the shortfall in grain supplies experienced by the Soviet Union in the early part of 1980 and the occasional difficulties in obtaining supplies thereafter had any impact on Soviet policy towards its occupation of Afghanistan. The circumstantial evidence is that the main effect of the embargo in the Soviet Union was to add strength to the case of those arguing for further agricultural investment and the reassertion of the principle of self-sufficiency.

The ending of the embargo policy, amidst acrimony and dissent within the American Administration in the summer of 1981 did not herald a new period of large-scale trade between the two countries. As Table 4.11 shows, despite the increasing scale of import needs the Soviet Union has progressively diversified its sources of supply, with reports suggesting that in 1982/3 it bought little more than the minimum six million tons specified in the 1975 agreement. The figure rose out of necessity to meet the much increased import requirement of 1984/5 but even then the Soviets managed to find 60% of their requirements from other sources.

The Soviet policy has of course been reinforced and assisted by the willingness of other exporters from the Canadians to the French to provide supplies on advantageous terms.

The Soviet trading strategy has had serious consequences for the United States. Instead of leading to a general switching of the pattern of trade with American grain taking markets previously held by those now supplying the Soviet Union, the prospect of Soviet purchases has actually stimulated production in some countries, particularly Argentina, where output of wheat rose from 5 million tons in 1977 to an estimated 14.5 million tons in 1982 as trade with the Soviet Union rose sixfold. The net addition to world supplies has inevitably contributed to the decline of the world price — a price which has considerable influence on the earnings of the US farmer, and the burden of agricultural support on the US Treasury.

Soviet trading policy has been confirmed by the new grain agreement, signed in July 1983. Under its terms the minimum

Table 4.11: USSR Grain Imports from Major Suppliers

	1976/ 77	1977/ 78	1978/ 79	1979/ 80	1980/ 81	1981/ 82	1982/ 83	1983/ 84	1984/ 85
Total	10.3	18.4	15.1	30.4	34.0	45.0	32.5	31.5	57.2
Of which:									
USA	7.4	12.3	11.2	15.2	8.0	15.4	6.2	10.4	22.3
Argentina	0.3	2.7	1.4	5.1	11.1	13.3	9.6	6.9	8.1
Australia	0.5	0.3	0.1	4.0	2.9	2.5	1.0	1.7	3.2
Canada	1.4	1.9	2.1	3.4	6.8	9.2	8.8	6.3	8.4
EEC	0.2	0.2	0.2	0.9	1.2	2.4	3.7	3.8	7.8

Source: International Wheat Council, *Market Report*, various issues.

volume of assured purchases is increased from six to nine million tons per year over the next five years 1983–8. For American farmers burdened by stocks and the prospect of excess supplies that is a very limited consolation when set against the regular sales of 15 to 20 million tons achieved in the late-1970s. Even to win that concession American negotiators were forced to concede that grain would not be used as a weapon of economic diplomacy, that supplies would be maintained in all conditions short of outright conflict, and that the clause in the 1975 agreement permitting the United States to cut off supplies completely in the event of a shortage should not appear in the new agreement.

Although the collection of long-term agreements, including the new agreement with the United States, confirms the need to import over 20 million tons per year of one form of grain or another for the foreseeable future and therefore represents an indictment of the Soviet agricultural system, they also confirm that the Soviet Union is both willing and able to exploit its trading power in what has become a buyer's market. The diversification of sources of supply seems likely to continue but it is not the only consequence of the 1980 embargo and the threats of trade sanctions made so often over the last decade.

Although much effort has been devoted in the Soviet press and elsewhere to playing down the impact, it is clear that the cutoff of supplies in 1980 did bring home to the Soviets their potential vulnerability. Introducing the new food programme in May 1982 Mr Brezhnev is reported to have said:

> Soviet policy proceeds from the need to reduce imports of foodstuffs from capitalist countries. As you know the leadership of certain states is striving to turn ordinary commercial operations such as grain sales into a means of putting pressure upon us.[15]

The 1980 embargo led to some small-scale distress slaughtering of livestock, and forced the Soviets to run down stocks to particularly low levels. A sustained embargo from the United States, or a briefer but more co-ordinated embargo adhered to by Canada, the EEC, and Australia (if not Argentina) would leave the Soviets very short of supplies, and might force them to slaughter cattle on a significant scale in a year of poor domestic crops. Immediate food supplies would not therefore be threatened but the strategy of improving diets, and providing meat to Soviet citizens would be set back for many years. Although the threat is not an immediate one, Soviet policy seems likely to be to continue to seek diversified sources of supply, to continue to regard agriculture as 'one of the most important component parts of the Party's economic strategy for the next decade'[16] and to continue to devote resources to its own production sector in the hope that imports can once again be reduced to such a level that the temptation to use grain as a political weapon is removed. After a period in which imports became a respectable and accepted part of the Soviet strategy, the 1980 embargo may therefore have revived the Soviet commitment to self-sufficiency as an objective, whatever the short-term circumstances.

Conclusion

For those, particularly the groups within the US Administration who at times over the last decade have dreamt of the development of a permanent Soviet market for US grain exports of 50 million tons or more providing a potential solution to the problems of expanding US production and the resulting surplus, the conclusion must be depressing if no longer surprising.

Even the new Grains Agreement will not relieve the gloom since the level of minimum purchases has been raised only modestly by the Soviets.

The Soviet Union has not escaped its dependence on imports, and shows little sign of being able to do so for the immediate future. What it has done, however, in response to the embargo and world market conditions is to show that power in the grain market does not lie on the side of the supplier alone, and that importing countries, particularly if they control information and purchasing decisions, can do much not only to relieve their own position, but also dictate the fortunes of other participants.

Notes

1. The debate is not limited to the United States. Under the heading 'Food is Power' *The Times* leader of 26 February 1982 thundered, 'We ought not to be protecting the Soviet leaders from the consequences of their unwillingness to change from a warfare state to an agrarian one . . . The Soviet Union knows perfectly well that its dependence on our food production is a major and constant source of

weakness. We should show them that we know too'.

2. *Financial Times*, 27 May 1982.

3. Karl-Eugen Wadekin, 'Soviet Agriculture's Dependence on the West'. *Foreign Affairs*, May 1980.

4. A. Nove, in A. Brown (ed.), *Soviet Policy for the 1980s*, Macmillan, 1982.

5. 'Brezhnev's Report on the Food Programme', *Summary of World Broadcasts*, BBC, 26 May 1982.

6. P. Desai, 'Estimates of Soviet Grain Imports in 1980 and 1985', IFPRI Research Report 22, 1981.

7. Dan Morgan, *Merchants of Grain*, Viking, 1979.

8. 'The Food Programme of the USSR for the Period up to 1990', *Summary of World Broadcasts*, 4 June 1982. The programme remained unchanged under both Andropov and Chernenko and is still current policy.

9. Wadekin, ibid.

10. Ibid.

11. While the Soviet Union appears to have had no major difficulty in financing its imports, it is clear that increasing real grain prices over a sustained period relative to other goods and in particular to Soviet exports would create balance of payments problems, and is likely to be one of the concerns motivating current Soviet policy. Agricultural goods accounted for a third of all imports in 1984.

12. R. Gilmore, *A Poor Harvest*, Longman, 1982.

13. D. Gale Johnson, *Soviet Impact on World Grain Trade*, British North America Committee, 1977.

14. E. Lindell, 'Multinational Companies and the Grain Embargo', *Food Policy*, August 1982. For a thorough and expert discussion of the 1975 Grain Agreement and its development see Porter, *The US-Soviet Grain Agreement*, Cambridge University Press, 1985.

15. *International Herald Tribune*, 26 May 1982.

16. 'Food Programme', *Summary of World Broadcasts*, BBC, 4 June 1982.

5   THE GRAIN TRADE AND THE FAILURE OF INTERNATIONAL CONTROL

For those with tidy minds favouring neat theories and orderly patterns of behaviour a study of the world's agricultural economy can only be a source of disillusion and despair.

In the fiscal year of 1983 the US Treasury contributed over 20 billion dollars to the support of the US farm sector. The main slice of that expenditure went on a single programme — the Payment in Kind scheme which took grain acreage out of production and compensated farmers by releases of stocks from the overfull public granaries. Though stocks of coarse grain fell, by 70 million metric tons worldwide according to the International Wheat Council, few of the benefits went to the American farmer. Grain production rose in Argentina, Europe, Australia and the Soviet Union and the rewards of partial stabilisation of the market for corn if not for wheat accrued to farmers far distant from the American Mid-West.

The Soviet Union, which only two decades ago was a net exporter of grain — to its allies and to India — and which six decades ago proclaimed its faith in self-sufficiency as a matter of political principle, imported some 57 million tons of grain (including ironically a small amount from India) in the 1984/5 crop year as well as a substantial volume of meat. At the same time Chinese production increased in line with the government's target but imported grain remained a key element of policy — feeding the coastal cities and the army and leaving a little more of the country's indigenous supplies to be used as rewards and incentives for peasants too little inspired to effort by ideology alone.

In Britain, once a significant and secure market for good-quality North American grain, the impetus provided by the high guaranteed prices of the Common Agricultural Policy brought a bumper crop and the third successive annual export surplus — a trade position unprecedented since Sir Robert Peel as Prime Minister scrapped the protectionist Corn Laws in the 1840s.

In the same crop year only two thousand miles away from the UK tens of millions went hungry and hundreds of thousands died in front of the world's television cameras. At even generous consumption levels the stocks of grain held by the European

Community at the end of 1984 could have fed every individual in Ethiopia and the Sudan for half a century.

This combination of circumstances — part farce and part tragedy — arises not from the operation of any inviolable economic law but from the interplay of domestic political forces which determines the development of agriculture in each separate country. The combination of protection and subsidy ensures that the world market, whether in times of surplus or shortage is treated as a residual, used by producers and consumers alike as a means of stabilising their own supplies and not as a price mechanism indicating the required adjustment in either supply or demand.

In an illogical and economically inefficient market, international regulation and organisation is noticeable by its absence. Yet for specific exporters and importers the importance of the grain trade is growing. Trade conflicts are worsening and security of supply is only half assured by surpluses.

If new attempts are to be made to establish order in the grain market an understanding both of the failures of the past and the context of the immediate future is necessary.

The Growth of Trade

The total volume of world trade in agricultural products has grown by almost 4 per cent per annum for each of the last three decades. Trade in grain alone grew by 8 per cent per annum on average during the 1970s and was 190 per cent higher in 1980 than two decades earlier, against a total production increase of only 70 per cent over the same period. By 1980 the grain trade, led increasingly by trade in feed grains for consumption by livestock, accounted for over a quarter of non oil bulk shipping trade. The expansion of trade in manufactures which for so long overshadowed agricultural developments was matched, and even surpassed in the 1970s by the growth of the grain trade.

The changes in the pattern of trade have been as significant as the changes in total volume. The shift in the position of the Chinese and the Soviets has been balanced by the effects of the Common Agricultural Policy in Europe, and the effect of technological advances. The EEC, after decades during which its member states were among the world's largest-scale importers, has achieved not just self-sufficiency but also the capacity to become a major exporter of grain. Restructuring and major gains in productivity as well as a generous support price policy on the part of the government have encouraged a continuing growth in US output almost all of which, since 1970, has been exported. Japan and a few of the more rapidly growing Third World countries with the resources to feed their growing population have accounted for a major proportion of that new trade.

Although the bulk of world grain output is consumed where it is produced, with less than a fifth of total output traded in an average year, the changes in the pattern and the scale of trade have established it as an important factor, politically as well as economically, for the countries concerned. In some US states as much as 70 per cent of farm income is now earned by exports. Grain partially offsets the adverse US trade balance. Soviet imports have allowed the continued development of a livestock sector vital to the provision of food supplies to the Soviet consumer.

Growth in volume and importance, however, has not been matched by stability. During the period of trade expansion, year to year volumes have fluctuated widely. Trade in food grains grew by 4 per cent per annum between 1960 and 1980, with an annual average variation from trend of 7 per cent. The comparable figures for feed grains were 7.6 per cent per annum and 5.1 per cent, while the annual variation for all agricultural products was only 2.6 per cent, and for total trade as low as 1.5 per cent. Within the period the average annual variation of consumption from trend worldwide doubled in the 1970s as against the 1960s.

The fact that traded grain is in essence marginal — a reflection of surplus or deficit in individual countries — and that production is particularly vulnerable to adverse weather conditions and disease, accounts of course for the volatility. The grain trade is unlikely ever to be stable or predictable but unpredictability is enhanced by the lack of international organisation or regulation of the trade. In common with international agricultural trade in general the grain trade has remained immune to pressure for liberalisation, and equally immune to suggestions of international management in the form of reserve stock holdings, price floors and ceilings, or a full-scale commodity agreement.

Concern with the issue is of course nothing new. The attempts to bring agriculture and grains under the control of the General Agreement on Tariffs and Trade go back to the 1940s while efforts to create an effective International Wheat Agreement go back to the 1930s. The fear of shortage and famine in the 1970s generated numerous proposals in the area of food security, and repeated calls for a new global food regime but beyond a widening and strengthening of the intellectual debate little came of such proposals. The trade remains illiberal, erratic and unmanaged.

In the United States and the European Community the pressures of protectionism, and the strength of the farm lobby, coupled with achievements of technical progress which other sectors would envy, have generated large and growing surpluses of supply over demand. Grain consumption per capita in both regions has plateaued while grain output per capita has accelerated. The consequence has been that the US volume of exports has risen by 60 million tonnes in a decade and now accounts for 25 per cent of production (40 per cent of feed grain production). At the same time the farm policy of the EEC has left the Community with an exportable surplus in grains likely to grow, according to recent forecasts, to well over 25 million tons per year by 1990.

Worldwide, effective demand has not matched that growth. Prices have declined sharply from their peak in the mid-70s. Fears of supply insecurity and the perception of grain as a strategic commodity have encouraged the development of grain production in many countries, in some cases regardless of the true economics of the situation. Both the US and to a much greater extent the EEC have been forced to subsidise their exports — the EEC by as much as 100 per cent of the world price, contributing to the financial burden on the Community caused by export restitutions to agriculture of 6,082 million units of account, 38 per cent of the Community's agriculture budget in the 1983 financial year.

In the recent past that situation and the competition for markets has become sharper, even bitter, and agricultural trade disputes, whether between Europe and the United States, America and Japan, or Australia and the EEC, have occurred with increasing regularity.

In such circumstances it is worth examining the reasons for the failure of past attempts to liberalise and regulate trade and questioning whether there is indeed a way forward which does not involve a war of subsidies and an even greater misallocation of resources.

The Record

For four decades the GATT rounds of trade negotiations have failed to penetrate the agricultural sector. While tariffs on manufactured goods have been reduced and codes of practice developed, the agricultural sector has stubbornly remained beyond the reach of the general tide of liberalisation. Tariff levels (in one guise or another) have actually increased and the effect of national measures on international trade has grown as that trade itself has expanded.

A major study of agricultural trade relations written a decade ago analysed the circumstances which brought this about:

> in essentially all countries, and for a variety of economic, security, social and political reasons the agriculture industry is supported, planned and managed to a degree which is without parallel in any other sector of the economy, with the possible exception of defence industries. . . . Agriculture ministers and officials regard external demands to lower import barriers as a troublesome and unwarranted interference with the national farm programmes for which they are responsible . . . [Consequently] agriculture trade liberalization is an area which has had meagre success. Every country has a compelling reason to give primacy to supporting some sector of its agriculture over its general obligations under GATT and for the most part other members have acquiesced.[1]

The world market in grains, important though it is to all sides, has therefore remained merely the residual result of the sum of the national policies of the major trading nations — importers and exporters. Trade barriers and in particular the variable levies of the EEC prevent the transmission of market signals, through price changes. At the same time the willingness of the United States to accept its former responsibility for managing the market by absorbing fluctuations has sharply declined. Given this context it is remarkable that the system has operated without a serious breakdown for the bulk of the last decade.

From the immediate post-war years onwards, first in the Havana Charter and then within GATT, the advocates of trade liberalisations have fought a series of bureaucratic and political battles in order to include agricultural trade within the framework of the General Agreement. In the early rounds the pressure for liberalisation came almost exclusively from the exporting countries — Australia, New Zealand and Canada prominent among them. In Europe the concern was to redevelop an agricultural sector destroyed by war and to avoid farm incomes falling totally out of line with incomes in the prospering industrial sectors. With the historic traditions of protection in almost all the European countries other than Britain, this meant that liberalisation of agricultural trade did not figure high in any list of European priorities.

Nor was the United States a noted advocate of liberalisation. The Agricultural Adjustment Act of 1933, one of the early New Deal measures to secure American agriculture and the livelihood of the American farmer remained on the statute book and the American administration was far from confident that the removal of import duties and quotas, which the general application of GATT rules to agriculture would imply, would benefit their farmers in the face of foreign competition. When, in the mid-1950s, agriculture did become nominally subject to GATT rules the USA sought and obtained a waiver to permit the continued used of the AAA provisions. In the forum of GATT where the American voice had been the strongest advocate of open trade in general, the waiver marked the end of aspirations for a full incorporation of agriculture into the new trading system.

In the words of one of the most respected of American commentators on agricultural trade relations:

The US has a number of farm programmes that clearly violate the letter or spirit of GATT.- Some of the provisions have no significant economic effect but yet are retained in spite of their violation of GATT Article XI. Other provisions that violate GATT do have significant economic effects. Frankly it is relatively easy to see why foreign officials react with skepticism when we loudly proclaim our support for liberal trade in agricultural products while we have a GATT waiver so that we can maintain import quotas on dairy products since our dairy price support programmes are not designed to 'restrict domestic output or marketings' of milk. Quite the contrary, the programmes are in fact designed in such a way that milk production is encouraged . . . As things stand now, it is rather easy to characterise the US position as one of favouring trade liberalization for products that we export but also one that is highly restrictive for imported products that are competitive with our own production. This is something of a caricature — but not very much.[2]

The fact that both the European Community and the United States favour only selective liberalisation rather than the general extension of the principles of free trade to agriculture has kept the issue beyond the reach of GATT.

The GATT articles of agreement therefore include special provision to allow for the fact that agriculture is not subject to the general rules of free trade. Article XVI prohibits subsidies 'including any form of income or price support, which operates directly or indirectly to increase exports or to reduce imports of any product'. Article XI declares that 'no prohibitions or restrictions other than duties taxes or other charges shall be instituted or maintained on imports or exports'. But, with the common agreement of both the United States and the Europeans, these declarations have been hedged by a whole series of exceptions and escape clauses which have had the effect of destroying the meaning of their basic thrust.

The result is that the degree of protection tolerated in the post-war period has become entrenched and apparently irremovable.

The record since then has been of successive attempts to introduce codes, to regulate tariff levels and, in the 1970s and in particular in the Tokyo Round, to set limits to the impact of non-tariff barriers, export subsidies and countervailing duties. It is certainly arguable that the reach of the attempts has shortened over time. The early attempts to treat agriculture on a par with other trade in manufactured goods, which sought a parallel reduction of tariff barriers with the ultimate aim of free trade, soon came to appear unrealistic. By the 1960s when the setting of price levels within the EEC had established the Community's commitment to a policy of agricultural protection and output growth the problem for GATT was arguably to prevent conflicts in agricultural trade adversely affecting other trade liberalisation as they threatened to. On the eve of the Kennedy Round the US threatened to refuse to conclude any part of the negotiations until 'equitable tariff and trade agreements have been developed for agricultural products.'

A decade later in the run up to the Tokyo Round negotiations another US trade representative wrote:

We should make clear to our partners right from the start that we are seriously prepared to withdraw from GATT and return our import duties to more protective levels if we cannot arrive at a satisfactory trade and monetary settlement including liberalization of the grain-feed-livestock sector along with appropriate additional settlements for other agricultural commodities.

Though the threats were never fulfilled, the danger of fundamental damage to wider trade relations was perceived and every effort made to separate agricultural and non agricultural negotiations, with the aim of reducing the scope for potentially dangerous attempts to link the two.

The Tokyo Round in particular confirmed the earlier reluctant acceptance of the status quo and the implicit recognition that agricultural trade would not be liberalised. Despite much rhetoric the CAP 'emerged virtually unscathed from the negotiations and the levy system thus received the final approval of the contracting parties.'[3] By the late-70s the GATT approach to agricultural trade was clearly to limit the development of new distortions and trade barriers rather than to seek the removal of those already in existence. The code on subsidies and countervailing duties applies to both agricultural and non-agricultural trade, establishing a clear incentive for the EEC as a large exporter of industrial goods to accept some limitation of its freedom of action in relation to the subsidisation of agricultural exports. Under the code, export subsidies on primary products are not to be applied when the exporting country would gain more than an equitable share of world export trade in these products.

The implicit legitimisation of export subsidies (and the other mechanisms of the CAP) short of the point where they shift the current pattern of trade and the vagueness of the definitions in the restrictive part of the code indicate the small amount of progress made. The challenge now before GATT panels, and the continuing French pressure for an explicit European export policy, illustrate the unresolved problems. The issue of export subsidies was the central issue of concern at the GATT ministerial meeting in November 1982 with a new proposal from the Australians for a standstill on trade distorting measures and a review of the GATT clause on subsidies with the aim of extending GATT scrutiny to cover measures of domestic assistance.

That this was the most radical proposal under consideration is perhaps indicative of the extent to which agricultural trade has, in the words of the *Financial Times*, 'slipped away from GATT' to a degree comparable to the textile sector, 'which has been hived off with built-in and legally sanctified restrictions on trade. The difference between the two is that there is no separate agreement for agriculture: the trading nations have simply constructed their own policies in the loopholes of GATT.'

It is certainly clear in retrospect that the EEC proposal at the beginning of the Kennedy Round for consolidating (and effectively freezing) the levels of support offered to agriculture through all the various devices available (the *montant de soutien*) was perhaps the nearest that GATT came to success in agricultural trade. The institutionalisation of protection which it implied and the lack of anticipation of the long-term effects on production of EEC support price levels led to its rejection by the American negotiators and no similar scheme has since been advanced.

Agriculture and the grain trade in particular have resisted the efforts of liberalisers for the last thirty years for three main reasons.

First, and most significant, is the 'special' importance attached by national governments to the farm sector and their consequent commitment — in the case of Europe, the Communist bloc, some developing countries and in different way, the USA — to protectionist devices to secure a greater degree of self-sufficiency and a higher level of income in the farm sector and the rural community it supports than would be the case if protectionist devices were removed.

Tim Josling, though sceptical of the claim for special status, has summarised the reasons why the claim has succeeded:

> Agriculture is the only sector which (i) provides an essential human need, (ii) is subject to erratic output variations on account of the vagaries of the weather, (iii) employs thousands of small businessmen in rural areas where other employment opportunities are scarce, (iv) has its own government ministries with deep seated involvement in economic and social programmes, and (v) exhibits a tendency to impose on itself stresses through the adoption of new technology which requires a significant resource adjustment to alleviate.[4]

It is clear though that agriculture is not the only sector for which special case status can be claimed, nor the only sector with a powerful lobby capable of outweighing the less organised consumer case, and that there must be other related reasons why trade liberalisation has so noticeably failed. The absence of a clear mutuality of interests — achievable through liberalisation and capable of overriding the strong domestic pressures for protection — has been of significant importance.

In contrast to the majority of other sectors the major obstacle to open trade has taken the form not of tariff barriers as such but rather a complex set of non-tarriff barriers which are not susceptible to easy measurement or to percentage reductions in the traditional GATT way. The non-tariff barriers vary from one country to another and are not easily equated. Given the inherent uncertainties of production and trade requirements the potential benefits and costs of liberalisation are not easily estimated. Agricultural policy is also so clearly a domestic matter with side effects on trade that significant liberalization would unavoidably impinge on the sovereignty of domestic policy making in a way few other GATT measures do. Given that most exporters do not have an explicit trade policy but rather export as a consequence of the effect of domestic policies on supply and demand, the problem is particularly difficult for an international institution to deal with.

The third reason for the lack of progress is that the main participants in GATT discussions — the EEC and the USA — have for most of the period found the existing arrangements tolerable if not optimal. The GATT negotiations on agriculture which have taken the form in essence of an Atlantic dialogue have been characterised by rhetoric, but rhetoric which has not disguised the fact that trade has continued to grow — providing scope until very recently for expanding production and relatively secure farm incomes. Looking back at the 1950s and 1960s, Warley concluded that 'the international effects of national agricultural policies were adverse but not intolerably so'.

Such a judgement is valid for the 1970s also. The USA has lost much of the European market for its grains which existed in the 1950s and 1960s but has found new markets for grain outside Europe, and new agricultural trade markets for other products in Europe which assure it of a very favourable trade balance. The benefits of liberalisation (which would have affected US agricultural imports as well as its exports) were, and are, at best uncertain and questionable. Recent studies suggest that a general liberalisation of Japanese and European agricultural policies would have a significant impact upon the distribution of income within the US agricultural sector but only a minor impact on the total. Producers of some commodities (e.g., wheat) would gain while producers of others (e.g., soyabeans) would lose. The net income gain to US agriculture would be relatively small. Considering the impact upon US customers and the rest of the economy there might not be a net gain.

Market Regulation

Just as attempts at liberalisation have been unsuccessful, so too have the various proposals for regulation and for partial or total control of the grain markets by some external authority. The attempts have taken many forms over the last three decades and the debate surrounding the issue has revived since the fears of 'food crisis' in the mid-1970s. Attempts at control can be divided into three distinct categories: (a) the attempt to establish a full-scale wheat or grains agreement, covering all aspects of trade internationally; (b) attempts to improve food security — through food aid conventions, internationally held reserves, food financing facilities or aids to production in vulnerable areas; (c) the quite distinct efforts by the major grain exporting countries to divide the market between them and to set an effective floor price.

All three have been pursued in the last decade but only the second, which falls outside the commercial arrangements under consideration here, has made any degree of progress, and that very limited.

The most comprehensive of the plans put forward in recent years for the management of the international grain trade has centred on the establishment of internationally controlled stocks and the extension of the International Wheat Agreement with the aim of stabilizing the markets for wheat and coarse grains and providing security of food aid supplies.

International Wheat Agreements have existed in one form or another for fifty years. The origins of the first agreement lay in the chaotic world market conditions of the 1920s and early 1930s, when the instability of economic conditions caused extensive competition for the remaining markets, particularly the markets of Western Europe between the United States and the exporting countries of central Europe. By 1933 in the context of a series of New Deal measures, and government intervention to secure agricultural incomes, the American administration which had held out against other pressures, finally accepted the principle of world market management, with export quotas, firm import commitments, and production limits, for each of the main participants in the market, including the United States itself. The Wheat Agreement as originally conceived included all these provisions plus a pegging of the international price of wheat to the gold standard in the hope of securing prices and gradually eliminating tariffs.

But the agreement did not hold. The abandonment of the Gold Standard disrupted the interlinked agreements on prices and quotas. The burden of surplus stocks was such that few could resist the temptation to exceed quotas and undercut prices. By 1935 the Agreement was virtually inoperative.

The years from 1935 onwards were spent trying to develop an effective multilateral agreement which assured supplies to importing countries and markets to exporters at equitable and stable prices. The agreement which came into force in 1949 was maintained for two decades but the loss of market stability at the beginning of the 1970s broke the consensus which had existed and left the IWA and the Wheat Council which services the agreement as no more than a channel of information — important though that role has been.

The attempt to use the IWA as the basis of market regulation in the interests of stability and security arose out of the 1974 World Food Conference and the earlier FAC international undertaking on world food security. Five years of discussion produced no agreement and though periodic attempts have been made to revive the issue since the breakdown in 1979 the only achievement has been the extension of the existing (limited) agreement and the increased commitments to food aid in the 1980 Food Aid Convention.

The negotiations focused on the details of a proposal to establish a clear set of guidelines for action in the event of either rising or falling prices. The 'action points' ranged from a close review of the market, to a commitment to purchase or release stocks. Beyond this general framework of discussion few points of detail were agreed. 'There were substantially different views on the price levels for reserve stock action. Developing country importers generally supported accumulation and release prices of $130 and $160 per metric ton respectively and major exporters generally supported $140 and $210. Furthermore the size of reserve stock obligations was not established'.[5] Both the United States and the developing importers argued for a level of 25–30 million tons as a minimum; the European Community for some 15–20 million tons.

The arguments offered reflected the interests of the various participants in the context of their national agricultural policies. Exporters generally sought to increase world prices (or to avoid anything which might reduce them), importers to limit any such increase. Given the significantly greater efficiency of a system based on international rather than national stock holding, and the reduced cost of such a system, the developing countries had a clear interest in the success of the proposals limited only by the inability of the negotiators to agree on the division of the costs involved:

> The EEC being both an importer and exporter of grain took a relaxed view of the price stability problem. Since its own international grain markets were so thoroughly insulated from world price fluctuation the Community preferred a modest International Grain Reserve — modest in its implied financial obligations and requiring no modification of the elaborate internal pricing and external trading practices of the CAP.[6]

The United States was instinctively cool to the idea of stock management and particularly unhappy that the scheme further entrenched the CAP, requiring no change in its operations and no constraints on its future expansion. The USA sought a large stock level in order to spread the burden away from its own budget.

US-European conflicts, the difficulties of negotiating any agreement between seventy countries, the uncertain and ill-defined role of the Soviet Union, and finally the objections of the developing countries to the proposed price levels all delayed and in the end prevented agreement. World market conditions also contributed. The shift from scarcity (or the perception of scarcity) to surplus led the USA in 1977 through the establishment of the farmer owned reserve to assume the effective burden of stock holding without any international obligation. The concept of the problem and of the solution required altered while the negotiations were taking place to the extent that the assumptions on which the discussions began were eroded.

It is ironic that the very significant increase in stock levels in the last few years has not brought stability to the market. The growth of stocks has been, as ever, concentrated in the exporting countries who have consequently been forced to bear their cost. The absence of international control not only means that the stocks now built up would not necessarily be available to those in greatest need in times of chronic shortage but also that the nationally held stocks could be sharply reduced for purely national reasons — such as the cost — without reference to the international situation.

The risk seen so clearly a decade ago, that increasing reliance by less-developed countries on imports could lead to circumstances of crisis if those imports were not readily available, is as strong as ever.

Low prices have encouraged rather than discouraged dependence on external suppliers by some Third World countries. Few though can afford the investment necessary to build their own stocks 'to cushion them against price increases or market shortages . . . Most of them are experiencing severe balance of payments difficulties and are vulnerable even to relatively small price rises. But many cannot afford to hold larger stocks without international assistance.'

No greater progress has been achieved in the very different attempts to organise international trade in grain by the establishment of a common set of policies by the main grain exporting countries. The Canadians and Australians with strongly export orientated industries have long favoured attempts to set floor prices, and to limit the risks of competitive subsidies by a division of the market between them. Agreement on market shares, however, has always been elusive given the American aim of increasing export trade. The European Community, as exporter and importer, has conflicting interests and has consequently never fully embraced the idea. In addition to the problems of policing arrangements, and the provision of special deals for particular customers, such as the Third World importers, the main stumbling block has been the acceptance of a measure of external control over domestic production levels. As a recent study of the subject suggests, the achievement of high prices if passed on to the producer would make the imposition of controls on supply unavoidable.[7] All the factors which have militated against liberalisation in terms of the national sovereignty of agricultural policy making are raised again by such a proposal.

In the absence of international control, much of the management of the grain trade has devolved to the international grain traders — the five major companies (Cargill, Continental Grain, Louis

Dreyfus, Bunge and Andre). The nature of this management and the desirability of the concentration of market power in the hands of such a small number of private traders has become a subject of controversy. Richard Gilmore, a professional in the grain trade has written:

> A small cluster of companies now exercise a tremendous hold over domestic and international grain markets . . . An oligopoly of intermediaries now claims a disproportionate share of the profits in grain production, marketing and distribution. Dependence on the private grain traders has cost exporting and importing countries alike in terms of revenue foregone and unfavourable prices, and has made agricultural planning difficult.

In the absence of detailed analytical work, almost impossible given the secrecy of the companies' operations, it is difficult to assess how far their undoubted commercial power has influenced the pattern of trading. Undoubtedly that power is substantial, but economic and political factors have limited its use. The inability of the world's poorest people to buy, even in weak markets, has restricted trade potential. The desire for security both on the part of buyers and of sellers has encouraged government to government agreements at a bilateral level, leaving the grain companies to fulfil the role of shippers, rather than full controllers of all aspects of trade.

The excess of supply over effective demand in recent years has contributed significantly to the development of bilateral trade deals — reducing the proportion of traded grain available in the open market in any one year. In addition to the US-Soviet grain agreement of 1975, bilateral agreements have been signed by the USA, Canada and Australia. One of the propositions under consideration by the EEC is an export policy based on such bilateral agreements.

The attempt on the part of exporters to secure markets and thereby to provide guaranteed commercial outlets for their production, and on the part of importers to secure a guarantee of first call on supplies, even in times of supply shortage, is the result of the perceived instability of the world market and the desire of those involved to minimise their vulnerability to such instability. For both exporters and importers bilateral deals have become an extension of the system of national protection. They are unsatisfactory in global terms because of the risks they pose in times of shortage.

Although three times more grain, as a proportion of production, is now traded internationally than was the case in 1950, a substantial proportion of that is now accounted for by bilateral deals signed in advance. Since only those countries reasonably secure in their ability to pay for imports enter into such commitments it is the countries whose financial strength is less certain which must make do with the residual. The last five years have seen remarkable stability and indeed declining real prices, but a poor North American or European harvest coupled with a further heavy call on the market from the Soviet Union would push prices for available, unallocated supplies beyond the reach of a number of developing countries.

As things stand, the instability would emerge in the lower half of the two-tier world market. The relative vulnerability of developing countries is increased by the fact that livestock provides an additional buffer stock of food supply for the developed countries. These facts plus the vulnerability of concessionary supplies in such circumstances explain the continuing pressure for some form of food security regime. Scepticism about the likelihood of such a regime emerging is one of the main factors which in turn strengthens the view that protection and self-sufficiency policies, at almost any cost, are the only means of ensuring acceptable levels of security of supply. In the absence of wider agreements, bilateralism is also the central feature of trade negotiations.

As well as supply arrangements, questions of access, barriers to trade and marketing practices have tended to be handled directly between states with GATT doing no more than observing from the sidelines. The long-running and never fully resolved conflicts between the USA and the European Community have been contained by a mutual acceptance of specific policies in return for other particular trading advantages. Such arrangements are rarely explicit and often emerge only as a breach is threatened — as for instance when the Community looked likely earlier this year to impose taxes on corn gluten imports and to restrict access for products which have provided the USA with its balance of payments surplus in agriculture.

The conclusion must be that despite the apparent ease with which the agricultural trading system has dealt with the sharp changes in supply and demand for grain over the last decade it remains inefficient and weak. Increased trade, coupled with the nature of the trading arrangements, have made the world food system in Robert Paarlberg's words, 'more interdependent but less dependable'. The absence of stability has produced an overcompensation in terms of self-sufficiency which is highly inefficient in resource allocation. The 'stability' of the last few years has been rooted in the imbalance between protected production and the shortfall of effective demand. The immediate problems with which the trading system as it exists is unable to cope are the unrealised demands of many LDCS and the possible intensive competition among exporters for markets. The present system offers no limits to competitive subsidies (other than by bilateral agreement) and does 'nothing to stop Comecon or the EEC dumping their production instability on global markets'.[8]

The history of its past failure, however, as well as the evidence of current and increasing conflict, should not on the other hand be taken as suggesting that there is nothing which GATT can do. Although the prospects of extending a liberalising philosophy of international trade to the agriculture sector are negligible, the status and expertise of the GATT organisation does give it the chance to play a valuable if more limited role.

In Washington, Brussels and other centres of government, officials are now beginning to turn their minds to the next round of multilateral trade negotiations — christened in advance as 'the Reagan Round' by optimists in the US Administration. Agricultural trade should be placed on the negotiators' agenda, with the aim of establishing GATT as the central authority in agricultural trade matters, through a permanent Agriculture Committee.

Immediate liberalisation is a naive hope and the primary function of a new GATT authority must be more limited if a degree of realism is to be sustained. Though the acceptance of protection would undoubtedly be questioned by free trade purists the value of such an advance would lie in the establishment of a forum for regular international discussion of agricultural trade policy in place of the now dominant bilateral deals. Attempting to regulate trade relations is some distance from the original concept of GATT, particularly if the Committee found itself advocating one form of protection against another as a means of minimising the adverse effects on third parties, and especially on developing countries. In the longer term one might hope that the regulation would be more ambitious, leading beyond constraint to liberalisation, but that is a long way off and should be recognised as such.

To move to such a position, and to induce member states to participate fully in the work of an Agriculture Committee, GATT will have to accept the 'individual' character of the farm sector as a permanent and not a temporary phenomenon. If by a recognition of the reality that liberalisation is not on the agenda, GATT is able to limit the worst effects of protectionism in a sector of increasing rather than declining importance in world trade, the effort will be well worth while.

Notes

1. T. Warley, 'Western Trade in Agricultural Products' in Shonfield, *International Economic Relations of the Western World; 1959–71*, Oxford University Press, 1976.

2. D. Gale Johnson, *Agriculture and US Trade Policy*, Chicago, January 1983.

3. E. Bucholz, 'The Multilateral Trade Negotiations and Agriculture' in M. Tracy and I. Hodac (eds), *Prospects for Agriculture in the EEC*, Bruges, 1979.

4. T. Josling, *Agriculture in the Tokyo Round*, Trade Policy Research Centre, 1977.

5. Daniel T. Morrow, 'The International Wheat Agreement and LDC food Security' in *Food Security for Developing Countries*, ed. A. Valdes, Westview, 1981.

6. R. Paarlberg, 'A Food Security Approach for the 1980s' in *The US and the Third World*, Praegar for the Overseas Development Council, 1982.

7. A. Schmitz and A.F. McCalla, 'The Case of Grain Export Cartels' in T. Josling and McCalla, *Imperfect Markets in Agricultural Trade*, 1981.

8. M. Yudelman, 'Development Issues in the 1980s: Achieving Food Security'. Speech delivered in Melbourne, February 1982.

6 THE GRAIN TRADING COMPANIES

Susanna Davies

In most studies of the world grain trade, little or no direct reference is made to the role of the major grain trading transnational corporations (TNCs). This is despite the fact that five TNCs account for 85 to 90 per cent of American grain exports; 80 per cent of Argentina's wheat exports; 90 per cent of Australia's sorghum exports; 90 per cent of Canada's rapeseed exports[1] and 90 per cent of wheat and corn exported from the EEC. The five are Cargill, Continental, Bunge and Born, Louis Dreyfus and André Garnac. Until 1976, Cook Industries was a sixth member of the group, but was declared bankrupt and subsequently taken over by the Japanese firm Mitsui, in 1978. The figures in Tables 6.1 and 6.2 provide some partial evidence of the extent which these five corporations dominate world trade in grains.

This chapter seeks to trace the origins and characteristics of the five major grain trading TNCs, the reasons for their success in terms of market shares and the impact of their collective market dominance on the system of production and exchange and other participants.

The grain trading TNCs began as merchant houses in nineteenth-century Europe, with the exception of Cargill, the only one with American origins. Their evolution into huge TNCs is a chequered history of gradual expansion and success in surviving periods of collapse and subsequent concentration in the private grain trading sector. The industrial revolution and consequent urbanisation in Europe and the United States created the need for an increasingly comprehensive system of exchange of grains, giving rise to the emergence of numerous trading houses. The reasons for the success of the five companies under discussion — or, indeed, the comparative failure of many of their competitors — are complex and manifold.[2] Of particular significance was that all five exhibited, from an early stage, strong tendencies to expand operations on to a worldwide level and to become integrated into grain marketing systems: initially within domestic markets (through the acquisition of storage and handling facilities and the rental of transportation

Table 6.1: World Market Share of Grain Exports by Company

Estimates of exports by location on best available information

Country and Commodity	Year	Total exports (000 metric tons)	Major Grain Trading TNCS[a] Estimated %	Equivalent 000 metric tons
Argentina	1973/74			
Wheat		1,775	80[b]	1,420
Corn		5,874	50[b]	2,937
Sorghum		3,207	70[b]	2,245
Australia	1973/74			
Wheat		7,418	40	2,967
Barley		808	5	40
Sorghum		748	90	673
Oats		183	20	37
Brazil	1974			
Soyabeans		4,766	30[c]	1,430
Corn		886	30[c]	266
Canada	1973/74			
Wheat		12,007	20	2,401
Barley		3,559	90	3,203
Rapeseed		1,175	90	1,058
Flaxseed		465	90	418
Rye		138	90	124
Oats		24	90	22
EEC	1973/74			
Wheat		2,550	90	2,295
Corn		447	90	402

Notes: a. Continental, Cargill, Cook, Bunge, Dreyfus (and Anderson Clayton in Brazil). b. Figures based on licences issued to companies. c. Includes agents' deals.
Source: US Senate Subcommittee Hearings into MNCs, 1976; Gilmore, 1982.

equipment); and later on a global scale by establishing a network of subsidiaries in most countries which do not have state monopolies over grain trading. Even in these countries, there is company presence, as state traders rely on the TNCs for the actual physical importing and exporting of grains.

Their development has also been marked by the establishment of close links with other sectors which influence corporate activities: railway companies in the United States and Argentina in the nineteenth and early twentieth century; banks and other financial institutions; shipping and insurance companies. In recent years, this process of integration has taken the form of diversification into

Table 6.2: Major Grain Trading Companies' Participation in US Grain Exports, 1921 and 1970–75

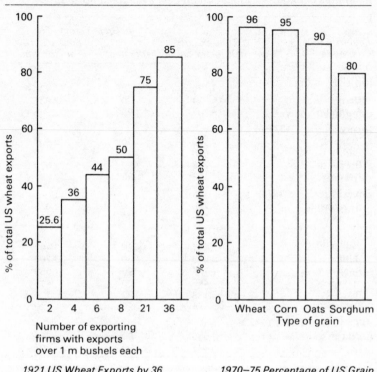

1921 US Wheat Exports by 36
Largest Companies

1970–75 Percentage of US Grain
Exports by 6 Largest TNCs

these sectors by the companies, thereby internalising many of the activities of which grain trading is comprised. Furthermore, increasing control over distribution channels and information regarding all aspects of production and trade have characterised these most successful grain traders' operations throughout the twentieth century.

The crash of 1929 and the depression and war which followed presented a host of disruptions to the grain traders. Those which survived the 1930s constituted a far more concentrated nucleus than was the case during the 1920s, when undercapitalised companies relying largely on credit and information had been able to flourish until their vulnerability was exposed by the collapse of the market.

The prevalent economic nationalism of the 1930s brought far

higher levels of state intervention into grain markets. This meant that the private trade was more restricted than it had been during the bout of pre-crash speculation and prosperity (although the United States retained a commitment to *laissez faire* policies and intervened in production rather than in trade). A further consequence of the 'slimming down' process of the 1930s was the realisation on the part of the survivors that undercapitalisation was too risky a position on which to base sustained growth and expansion. Those companies which had begun a process of downstream integration in the United States prior to the Second World War (especially Cargill and Continental) were in a unique position to benefit from the emergence of the United States as the leading grain power in the world in the aftermath of war. Despite regulation of shipments, the companies were able to service government-to-government contracts profitably, to benefit from subsidised transportation and to be leading participants in the huge increase in volumes of world trade as American production soared and world demand grew.

The 1950s and 1960s saw the development of a mutuality of interests between the companies and the American government, epitomised by PL480 sales which the companies serviced on a commissioned basis. This relationship was neither discussed nor questioned at any length in either government or academic circles until the so-called 'great grain robbery' in 1972, when the companies were responsible for selling unprecedented quantities of grain to the USSR despite the implications of such transactions for foreign policy considerations (see Trager, 1975).

The companies are renowned for their secrecy and anonymity. Private ownership of the five means that they are not required to publish annual financial reports. Consequently, all publicly available quantitative data about the companies is based on incomplete information. This is also true of estimates about corporate size (Table 6.3). It should be noted that corporate sales figures should be regarded with caution when used as a basis for comparison with manufacturing corporations. As the grain trading TNCs are primarily traders, sales are often of commodities which they have purchased at a price close to their own selling price. With manufacturing TNCs, raw material costs tend to be a far smaller proportion of their finished product prices.

Yet, since the great grain robbery these companies have increasingly become the subject of debate and have been alternatively criti-

Table 6.3: Estimates of Corporate Size and Growth of Major Grain Trading TNCs (US$ million)

Company	US sales	Total sales	Profits	Assets	Net income
Cargill	—	1978 11,600 1979 11,300	1979 121	1978 600+ 1979 3250	1978 121
Continental	—	1978 10,000 1981 7,000	—	—	—
Bunge & Born	1978 2bn	1975 2,800+	—	1975 450+ (US only)	—
Louis Dreyfus	—	1976 11,000	—	1976 300+	1976 1100 (US only)
Andre Garnac	1977 1.5bn	—	—	—	—

Company	Grain elevators	Feed milling plants	Oilseed processing plants	Futures Brokerage Office
Cargill	worldwide 385	worldwide 60	worldwide 28	—
Continental	US 70	US 24	worldwide 10	worldwide 34

Notes: + = at least or over; ———— = not available.
Sources: Burbach and Flynn, 1980; Moskowitz, Katz and Levering, 1980; Continental Grain Company, Tradax England Ltd, 1981; Gilmore, 1982.

cised and lauded by governments and public alike (US Senate Subcommittee Hearings on MNCs, 1976; Morgan, 1979; Gilmore, 1982). Much of this debate has been conducted at a highly subjective level and has consequently produced little rigorous analysis of the precise effects that these corporations exert on the world grain trade. On a more positive note, the debate has served to publicise the corporations (and their collective market dominance of the grain trade). Specifically, it has brought into question the validity of traditional studies of the trade which have tended towards country-by-country analyses (importers and exporters), which have focused attention on the state rather than the private sector as executors of undue market influence. The implicit assumption has been that the latter operates according to principles of free trade and is thus comprised of numerous independent traders. Hence, the market is seen to be a highly competitive forum in which supply and demand considerations determine price, trade flows and market performance. Although such analyses do place due emphasis on the impact of government policies and state trading on the operation of the free market, the private sector has not been similarly reappraised as a source of market imperfections (see, for example, Grennes, Johnson and Thursby, 1978). Alternatively, studies have tended towards the opposite extreme, interpreting the entire functioning of the grain trade as a conspiratorial alliance between the TNCs, whose strength is such that it overrides all other contributory factors and actors (see, for example, Burbach and Flynn, 1980). A corollary to this line of argument is the assertion that the TNCs and major (non-state trading) exporting governments act in complicity (either planned or unconscious), at the expense of producers, consumers and national interests (see, for example, Trager, 1975). None of these arguments provide a *comprehensive* explanation of the TNCs and their role in the world grain trade.

Existing theories offer very little insight into how best to analyse these corporations. Free trade theory does not yet account for a high concentration of buyers and sellers; nor specifically for companies whose function is *trading* rather than production and selling. Oligopoly theory is also inapplicable, as there is little evidence to support the idea that the TNCs act in collusion to determine prices artificially. Moreover, as corporate profitability is decided by the margins made on transactions, rather than by absolute price levels, their main objective is market expansion rather than seeking a constant set of prices. The companies have to live with price instability and are able to act as arbitrageurs. Arguments (expounded by critics of the TNCs) which interpret the TNCs as being the sole agents responsible for price formation in world grain markets ignore the subtlety and complexity of price determination in the grain trade and market behaviour more generally. The evidence to support the existence of high barriers to entry into world grain markets is far more convincing. Indeed, a key reason for the TNCs' domination of trade at the international level is the unwillingness and inability of potential competitors to assume the risks inherent in trading on the world market which is characterised by numerous endemic sources of instability.

Theories which have been devised to explain the growth and development of TNCs are also largely inapplicable to the grain traders as they are almost exclusively based on case studies of the manufacturing sector. For example, much discussion revolves around the motivation for foreign direct investment (as opposed to domestic production for export). In the case of the grain traders, location of production abroad is only relevant in the context of their diversified activities, which are peripheral to their main objectives and have developed as an extension of grain trading operations rather than as a basis for corporate expansion, *per se*. In a world of multiple importers and exporters, grain trading TNCs operate internationally for largely self-evident reasons.

Theories which have been expounded in the context of agribusiness TNCs (Arroyo, 1979; Goldberg, 1974) are more relevant, although a key distinction between the grain traders and their counterparts in other agriculturally-based sectors is that the former originated in the *distribution* of grains and have subsequently diversified into other related activities; whereas other agribusiness companies generally began in *productive* operations (often plantations). Yet the reduction in direct involvement in production by the latter in recent years and the diversification of all agribusinesses into processing and provision of inputs and services means that the points of confluence between the two are increasing. Theories of agribusiness diverge widely in their assumptions and conclusions and although useful in identifying general patterns of corporate behaviour and expansion, there is no single argument that can be applied wholesale to the grain trading TNCs.

The dearth of relevant theory provides strong support for the argument that the grain trading TNCs can only be understood if analysed in the context of the world grain trading *system* and not at a level of abstraction which disguises the extent to which the corporations are the *product* of the system, as well as exerting strong influences on it.

The world grain trading system may be defined as the sum of relations of production, distribution and consumption of grains in the international system. Although not administered by a formal institution, these relations form an identifiable pattern over time. The major actors in the system are TNCs and states; and the place at which they meet is the world market. However, the world grain trading system differs from the world grain market in that it also includes the downstream relations which TNCs and states have with national grain sectors, the producers and consumers within them and the internal relations of distribution in national grain marketing systems. Much of the success of the TNCs in terms of market shares may be attributed to their ability to constantly rationalise and adapt corporate strategies and development in response to changes in various parts of the world grain trading system. The flexibility of the companies, derived in large part from their transnationality, means that they are uniquely placed *vis-à-vis* other actors to operate in and profit from the system and changes within it.

Despite the fact that most theories of TNCs (and the characteristics of these corporations to which they give rise), are largely inapplicable in the case of the grain trading TNCs, there are several characteristics which they do share with their manufacturing counterparts. These can be summarised as follows:

(i) operations in more than one country (which may or may not involve actual production);

(ii) relatively large size in terms of financial resources in comparison with most domestically-based firms;

(iii) an ability to engage in intra-firm trade owing to the existence of subsidiaries in more than one country (and thus a potential to manipulate prices);

(iv) a tendency for advanced technological research and development, made possible by the size of the corporations;

(v) a tendency to diversify vertically, and horizontally on an international level;

(vi) highly centralised control structures, invariably based in the home country;

(vii) a tendency to operate in sectors which are highly concentrated and thus which may exhibit market imperfections.

The grain trading TNCs also exhibit a further set of characteristics which are the result of their historical development and the influences and demands placed on them (for successful expansion) by the world grain trading system. These may be summarised as follows:

(i) a primary function as *merchants* or *middlemen* rather than producers;

(ii) a consequential emphasis on operations in the *distributional* part of of the world grain trading system;

(iii) a tendency to expand up- and down-stream from this distributional base (rather than from a productive base, which is generally the case) and also a tendency to diversify into related activities (for example, grain processing, poultry and livestock, trading in other commodities);

(iv) control over market intelligence, which is unchallenged by other institutions (both private and public), which is closely guarded and upon which much corporate success depends;

(v) an unusually close relationship with certain national governments, owing to the dependence of the state on the corporations for assured food supplies or surplus disposal and the high level of state intervention in the grain sector;

(vi) a collective dominance of the world market despite the presence of many smaller national companies which are important within their domestic markets;

(vii) a consequential potential to influence world grain markets which is not based on oligopolistic price manipulation but rather, on a more complex set of relations derived from the corporations' vertical integration into the marketing system (and hence their substantial control over it). The grain market thus remains competitive, but the distribution of gains is concentrated.

These characteristics are derived from the corporate structures of the TNCs, which have developed with a primary aim of achieving vertical integration into the grain marketing system on a worldwide level. This means that the scope of the corporations' activities extends far beyond the 'actual' marketplace (such as the Chicago Board of Trade). It is important to note that as a general rule the

TNCs do not own land.[3] They are thus one step removed from production. Grain is acquired either through direct ownership of local elevators or from other traders and assembled at company terminal elevators. Market integration at the national level is achieved through the ownership and/or control (through leasing agreements) of extensive networks of storage, handling and transportation facilities. These networks operate successfully because of the ability of the TNC's to *co-ordinate* various parts of grain distribution and exchange, and to connect these distributional activities with related operations. In so doing, the companies can achieve economies of scale and the internalisation of multiple processes which provide them with competitive advantages over other participants in the market. The TNCs collectively own or control a substantial proportion of storage facilities in the United States and the EEC. For example, Cargill and Continental together own or lease 50 per cent of the total storage space at American ports (Morgan, 1979: p. 235). Internationally, Cargill has storage space of 5,200 million kilogrammes (Debatisse, 1979: p. 121). Much of this space, as with transportation equipment, is leased rather than owned outright, thereby reducing the capital costs of the companies and enabling them to lease only when required. Less obvious elements of market integration include links with financial and shipping institutions and companies on a worldwide level; and the provision of fertilisers, seeds and veterinary products to farmers via company-owned local elevators.

A key element of market integration is market intelligence, over which it is widely acknowledged that the TNCs exert a near monopoly. All five operate extensive international intelligence gathering and collating networks. The bases for the accumulation of information are the subsidiary companies of the corporations. These operate in all major importing and exporting nations and are thus well positioned to act as 'listening posts'. Information which affects the grain trade ranges from the specific — crop yield forecasts and planting decisions; the amount of grain in passage, its origin and destination; grain stocks; prices of each transaction for grain exchanges; the national supply and demand position and on the market trends — to the general — weather forecasts; political and economic climates in domestic and international arenas; secondary markets for freight, insurance, other commodities and grain-related goods, foreign exchange, and so on. The cost of the kind of information gathering network necessary to fulfill all these aspects is evidently phenomenal on a worldwide scale and is such that only the largest TNCs can afford it. The use of highly sophisticated telecommunications equipment enables the TNCs to disseminate the information as well as to accumulate it and hence to enhance profitability and expansion. As such, market intelligence is a major barrier to entry to competitors, from whom it is closely guarded at all times.

The integration of the TNCs into many national grain markets means that their trading activities are conditioned by the following factors:

(i) Their ability to acquire and store grain independently of actual sales.

(ii) Their ability to achieve economies of scale at all stages of their marketing operations, especially in transportation and storage. As transportation and storage costs constitute the major component of middlemen's operating costs, the capacity to reduce these is a crucial element in determining profit margins.

(iii) The transnationality of the corporations means that they are able to rationalise their trading activities on a worldwide basis. This includes their ability to use the very precise information they have on exchange rates to their own advantage (although, of course, exchange rates can be a considerable source of instability and hence increase the risks of trading); and the global rationalisation of freight costs, taxation payments and all other items of expenditure.

(iv) The worldwide market integration and diversification of the TNCs furnishes them with the capacity for intra-firm operations, if the open market is less attractive for any reason. For example, even though the majority of the freight used by the corporations is not their own, corporate expertise and operations do extend into this area.

(v) the size and level of diversification of the TNCs enables them to manage and spread the risks inherent in grain trading to a far greater degree than is possible for smaller, national traders.

(vi) The TNCs' access to credit is based on an international set of links with numerous financiers in many nations, which exceeds the capacity of national traders.

(vii) The market intelligence of the corporations which is derived from their transnationality and size (and hence the amount of resources that can be made available for information gathering), is unparalleled by other traders.

(viii) The transnationality of the corporations means that they are less restricted by national government regulations and allegiances than national companies. This, coupled with the reliance of many governments on the TNCs for market information and access, gives the TNCs a unique position of influence *vis-à-vis* states which is not replicated by national traders.

These characteristics combine to illustrate the reasons why the TNCs are more competitive than their national counterparts. Cargill's European subsidiary, Tradax (the operational base of which is in Geneva, although the headquarters are in Panama, for tax reasons), is an example of the benefits which can accrue from transnationality. Not only is Tradax Geneva able to profit from Switzerland's lack of formal exchange controls and limited corporate taxation; but it is also able to act as a co-ordinating office for all Cargill's non-North American trading activities. Transnationality and diversification make it possible to take advantage simultaneously of the numerous incentives which individual nations offer in respect of the various aspects of grain trading and related activities. Hence, in addition to Switzerland, the United States and Panama, Cargill can operate soyabean processing plants in Brazil, feed plants in Taiwan, poultry farms in Britain and numerous other operations.[4] By way of illustration of the extent of the TNCs' global activities, Table 6.4 shows the products and services of Cargill US and the corporate structure of Cargill/Tradax.[5]

Diversification of the TNCs has been a major element of corporate strategy in recent years. It serves three basic functions: to spread risks away from the fluctuations in earnings inherent in grain trading; it provides a means of investing profits productively in a business with a relatively low level of fixed assets and labour costs; and it enables the corporations to become increasingly integrated into grain trading and related businesses. All five TNCs are widely diversified, although Cargill and Bunge and Born more so than the other three. Louis Dreyfus has tended towards concentrating on shipping and financial services. Continental, employing profits made during 1972/4,[6] has engaged in an extensive diversification programme in recent years. Corporate diversification has been based primarily on an extension of the use of expertise required in grain trading; a desire to extend operations into other aspects of the grain sector; and a wish to improve integration into domestic

Table 6.4: Cargill: Corporate Structure and Activities
Cargill: US Products and Services

Poultry and Cattle Production
Poultry Products Department
Shaver Poultry Breeding
Farms
Dean Farms
Caprock Industries (feedlots)
MBPXL Corporation

Grain Processing
Domestic Soyabeans
Crushing Division
International Soyabean
Crushing Division (flour and corn wet milling)
Seaboard Allied Milling Corporation
Burrus Milling Department
Ross Industries
Protein Products Division (textured vegetables protein, blended foods)
Screven Oil Mill (cotton ginning)

Grain Marketing
Commodity Market Division (Grains and oilseeds)
Sugar Department Molasses Department
Flax/Sunflower Department Copra Department (coconut oil)
Producer Marketing Department (100 Country elevators, 32 terminal elevators, 13 port elevators)
Sylvania Peanut Co. Heinold Elevator Company
Hohenberg Brothers Co. (cotton merchandising)
Pan American Division

Transportation
Transportation Department, (1,500 covered hopper cars)
B&M Towing Co (23 liquid barges and 3 towboats)
Bargco Inc. Gulflow Inc.
Cargo Carriers Inc. (229 barges and 4 towboats)
Greenwich Marine Inc.
Midwest Towing Co. (124 barges and 5 towboats)
TriState Marine Service Company
Marine Purchasers Inc. Rogers Terminal and Shipping Corp. (Stevedoring services)

Farm Supply
Seed department
Nutrena Feed division
International Feed Department
Fertilizer Department
Waycrosse. Inc.
(manufacturer of fertilizer spreaders and farm equipment)

Financial/Tax
Cargill Investors Services (commodity futures commission merchants)
Bank of Ellsworth
Cargill Leasing Corporation
Horizon Agency Inc. (Insurance)
Horizon Underwriters (Insurance)
Summit National Life Insurance
Company Cargill Americas Inc. (Western Hemisphere Trade Corporation)
Cargill Export Inc. (Domestic International Sales Corporation)
Tenant International Sales Corporation (Domestic International Sales Corporation)

Miscellaneous
Chemical Products Division
North Star Steel Company
Zelrich Steel Company Inc.
C. Tennant Sons and Co. (metals, ores, plastics and electronic components)
Tennant Strapping Division
Aenco Inc. (production and operation of solid waste plants)
Salt Department
Watkins Salt Company
Leslie Salt Company
Silent Knight Security Systems Inc.
Venture Sprinkler Inc.
Cargill Lumber Company

Source: Gilmore, 1982.

Table 6.4 (contd.): Cargill: Corporate Structure and Activities

Cargill/Tradax Corporate Structure

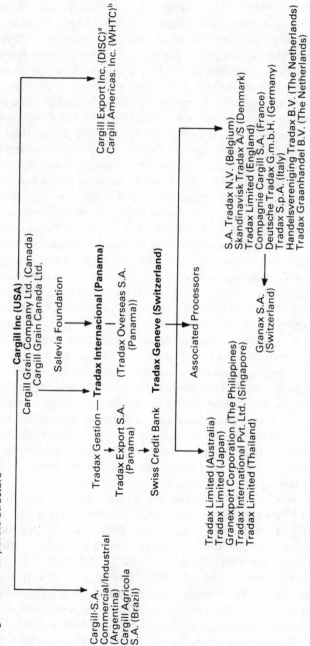

Notes: a. Domestic International Sales Corporation.
b. Western Hemisphere Trade Corporation
Source: Gilmore, 1982

marketing systems. Success in diversification has hinged not only on the extension of previously established skills, but also by innovation into areas which directly affect cost-effectiveness. Cargill, for example, moved into salt mining as a method of using transportation in both directions along the Mississippi River: grain to the Gulf of Mexico and salt on the return journey.

Diversification has taken place against a background of previously established transnationality: that is to say, prior to expanding operations into other areas, the TNCs had already established grain trading subsidiaries in many countries which provide a basis for further expansion into foreign markets. It should be noted, however, that diversification tends to occur in the home market first. Cargill, by far the most diversified of the five, now relies on non-grain trading activities for an estimated 60 to 70 per cent of earnings, against 40 per cent in 1970 (*Business Week*, 16 April 1979). Taken with merchandising of other commodities (cotton, scrap metal, ores, metals, concentrates, steel products, sugar, salt, coal), trading still accounts for the majority of corporate operations. But other areas of activity (in descending order of importance), include: agricultural products and commodity processing (for example, soyabean processing, flour milling, feed manufacturing, corn milling, poultry and egg production, cattle breeding, hybrid seed production, fertilisers); industrial products (for example, resins, chemicals, metal products); transportation (barge building, as well as bulk commodity handling and transporting); financial services (for example, leasing of farm equipment, construction and manufacturing machinery, insurance, futures brokerage services). Of Bunge and Born it is said in Brazil and Argentina that: 'Bunge gives the farmer his credit, sells him his seed and buys his grain. And when the crops are in, Bunge sells the farmer the rope to hang himself.'

The role of TNCs in the world grain trading system must obviously be considered in relation to other participants in the process of exchange. There are three basic categories of competitors for the TNCs: national trading companies, producer co-operatives and state traders. There is a temptation to overestimate the extent to which the TNCs dominate individual domestic markets, in which competition is often greater than aggregate world figures suggest. In the American market, for example, there are 40 to 50 other companies which regularly report sales to the United States Department of Agriculture. A notable development in recent years has been increasing participation by Japanese trading companies. It is clear from the characteristics of the TNCs enumerated, however, that many of the advantages which the TNCs are able to employ in their trading operations are not open to national companies on the basis of size and lack of transnationality. Similarly, producer co-operatives are far less flexible, as their marketing activities are constrained by the fact that they trade only those grains produced by their members and are obliged to conduct their operations on the basis of getting the highest price possible for those members. It is interesting to note that in 1973, American farmer co-operatives accounted for only 7.5 per cent of direct exports of grain, but 18 per cent of indirect exports (grain collected from producers but subsequently resold to the TNCs for export). By 1976, the figures were 7 to 8 per cent and 45 per cent respectively. Estimates are that as much as 70 per cent of the potential exports of the co-operatives are now sold to the TNCs (Schmitz, *et al.*, 1981: p. 32).

Relations between the TNCs and state traders are ambivalent. Although it is hard to generalise satisfactorily, the basic contradiction which exists between public and private sectors is surprising less in the conflict that arises, than in the degree to which the two collaborate in the grain sector. State trading nations are dependent upon the private traders to transport the grain (either to or from the domestic market) and, in many instances, for additional services including market access, information and storage facilities. There is strong evidence to suggest that the major state trading exporters (Canada and Australia) are seeing increasing incursions into their monopoly control of grain trading by the TNCs, in the form of country elevator acquisitions and the deregulation of certain products. In Canada, there is a lobby which argues in favour of total deregulation of grains, in the belief that the growth of the American export market has not been paralleled in Canada owing to government control which protects the interests of producers at the expense of wider economic considerations. On the importing side, the example of the Soviet state trading body Exportkhleb's deals with the companies in 1972, illustrates the degree of mutual dependence and co-operation between public and private sectors. In addition, the example of PL480 exports which are carried by private companies indicates that even in non-state trading nations, government policies relating to grain require the services of the private sector.

The precise relationship between the government (whether a state trader or not) and TNCs obviously varies from country to country and detailed analyses of this relationship can only be conducted at this level. In general, however, it may be argued that the TNCs have advantages over all other participants in the exchange of grains because they alone are designed exclusively for the purpose of operating in and benefiting from the world grain trading system, without the constraints implicit in having to operate to serve particular (and often conflicting) interests other than corporate growth.

Relations between the TNCs and the state more generally have invariably been discussed using the example of the United States. Two broad schools of thought exist. Firstly, that the interests of the United States are best served by the private sector (critics argue that there is actual collusion between the government and the TNCs). Secondly (particularly in the aftermath of sales to the Soviets in 1972 and suspected sanction breaking in 1979/80), that the corporations act solely to promote their own interests which are inimical to national interests. The truth of the matter lies somewhere between the two opposing positions: namely, that at times interests are likely to converge and at others to be in conflict. If national interests are deemed to be best served by offering incentives to the TNCs, this may produce collusion. Yet there is little evidence to support the idea of this being a permanent and immutable alliance. In the case of other nations (without such a predominant influence over the world grain trade as the United States), generalisations are unconstructive. However, on a national case study level, it is invariably possible to identify some kind of alliance between the state (be it a state trader or not) and the TNCs which is based not on collusion as such, but rather on the desire to secure mutual and possibly reinforcing interests. The nature of this relationship is determined by what objectives are sought by both parties; the level of participation of the state in question in the world grain trading system; and the wider context of levels of national development. All discussions of this relationship must, however, be based on the recognition that no alternative to the TNCs exists at present. Moreover, there is no way of knowing how the world grain trading system would be managed in the absence of these corporations.

Most discussions of TNC/state relations come down to a matter of control in the final analysis. This is particularly important in the case of the grain trade owing to the political sensitivity of food supplies and the strength of farm lobbies in exporting nations. Despite attempts by the American government in recent years to increase the accountability of the corporations, little headway has been made. The grain traders, like all TNCs, are inordinately hard to legislate for within the confines of national jurisdictions. This is compounded in the case of the grain trading TNCs by their lack of fixed assets which have traditionally been the target for governments wishing to increase national control over international corporations.

Of particular interest in this context are the reasons why the United States, as the most powerful state by far in the world grain trading system and hence the best placed to challenge the power of the TNCs, continues to go along with the *status quo* despite the undoubted dominance of much of the system of exchange by the TNCs. The United States does not exercise its potential for countervailing power because the existing system suits American interests by, essentially, letting it have its cake and eat it. That is to say, the United States can appear simultaneously to support an economic order based on free trade and enterprise whilst also selling to state traders, negotiating bilateral agreements, implementing export subsidies and, when necessary, dumping surplus grain through food aid transfers. Thus, the United States is able to pretend to be a liberal free trader whilst at the same time employing protectionist and other interventionist measures which enhance its competitiveness. This is the manifestation of the TNC/state alliance in the American instance and is based, as always, on the procurement of mutual interests.

However, despite the influence of the TNCs in the world grain trading system, the temptation to see them as omnipotent must be resisted. States continue to exert a strong impact on the trade as well, through actual market intervention and government agricultural and food policies more generally. The precise 'balance of power' between the two is neither constant nor universal. Nor, indeed, are states and TNCs easily comparable as they are not like objects and consequently a reduction in the power of one does not necessarily mean a concomitant increase of that of the other, and *vice versa*.

The corporations must ultimately be assessed in the context of their role in and effects on the market. The degree to which corporate size, structure and strategies differentiate the TNCs from other participants in the market is highly significant. Yet to interpret the TNCs as being in exclusive control of the market (and thus in a position to manipulate prices) does not represent the reality of the complex process of price formation and market activity. The worldwide market is undoubtedly concentrated, but it does not follow from this that competition is absent. There are numerous examples of corporate malpractice (price manipulation, shortweighting, misgrading); but these tend to distract attention from the fact that the corporations' market influence is based on their position of being the only market participants which are designed exclusively to serve and benefit from world grain markets, unbeholden to any interests other than their own. Coupled with this is the flexibility with which their size and transnationality furnishes them. If they wish to engage in intra-firm trade, or to establish parallel futures markets, or to send false price signals to the American market after the close of EEC trading by manipulating the variable EEC levy (all of which they have been accused of); they are certainly in a position to do so. But, such practices are an expression of market influence rather than a cause of market dominance. Their superiority is based primarily on their integration into the worldwide marketing system from multiple domestic bases (and the intelligence network which connects them), and their consequential ability to rationalise trading operations globally, rather than on malpractice.

Yet, it is necessary to determine why, if the market is open and competitive, is the trade so concentrated in the hands of a few companies? Firstly, the power of the TNCs lies in their control over distribution in the grain trade. As argued above, their vertical integration into marketing systems, their transnationality, size in terms of financial resources and monopoly control over market intelligence mean that market control originates far beyond the confines of the actual marketplace. Thus, the fact that the market is open, allowing an infinite number of traders to participate, is largely irrelevant as small-scale traders have no chance of being able to compete with the TNCs at the global level. They cannot hope to exercise equivalent market power and hence the TNCs' control of markets is due not to malpractice but to their position of strength *vis-à-vis* other actors. Competition is greater in individual national markets than at the aggregate world level because some of the benefits of transnationality are less effective locally than they are at the world market level. Producer co-operatives particularly, and small national companies, are less well-equipped in financial and corporate structural terms to assume the risks of trading on world markets and cannot rationalise risk taking and trading globally. They cannot achieve the same economies of scale as the TNCs and are more limited by domestic constraints. Lastly, their access to worldwide market intelligence is based largely on the 'generosity' of precisely those competitors they seek to outwit — the TNCs.

The TNCs are necessarily examined against the background of no alternative to them readily presenting itself. In addition, there is the perennial problem of it being impossible to determine what the current world grain trade would be like in their absence. The TNCs are frequently argued to be the most preferable type of trading organisation as their commitment to commercial efficiency ensures optimum global trading efficiency; and their transnationality and status as 'commercial' bodies enables them to act as buffers between governments, thereby reducing the risks of food distribution being interfered with by political considerations (Bastin and Ellis, 1980: p. 49). This kind of argument is based on the assumption that trading efficiency automatically serves the interests of the greatest number. What it does not account for is the possibility of the TNCs acting in conflict with the interests of individual nations (some of which exert considerable market influence in their own right), or with the interests of other groups in the trading system, in terms of distribution of costs and benefits. However, alternative suggestions for organising the world grain trading system, most notably the establishment of an exporters' cartel (see Schmitz *et al.*, 1981), imply the likelihood of increasing this unevenness yet further. What is evident is that the corporations are sufficiently powerful to make effective national legislation to control them or to monitor their operations in the grain market exceedingly difficult to implement. Consequently, the temptation to analyse the world grain trade in terms of national policies and performance alone needs to be resisted. Similarly, studies which regard the TNCs as 'anonymous' and neutral participants in world grain markets require reassessment which will accord due importance to the corporations as key sources of influence.

The failure to attach due importance to the TNCs is particularly relevant in the context of reform of the world grain trading system which aims to overcome the paradox of the coexistence of surplus management problems for exporters and food insecurity for the world's poor. Invariably, suggestions for reform refuse to face up to the central issue at stake: namely, that the distribution of power in the world grain trading system is heavily weighted in favour of those actors who stand to benefit from the continuance of the *status quo*. The TNCs are the primary members of this group, with the objective of promoting increasing volumes of trade rather than concern for redistributive measures. It is unrealistic to persist with policy proposals and analyses which insist on either ignoring the role of the TNCs altogether or on taking it as given and therefore according them only passing reference and, in so doing, implicitly assuming that these TNCs are responsive and accountable to states and any policy changes they might seek to implement, either individually or acting together. The five TNCs which account for 85 to 90 per cent of world trade in grains have no need to be accountable to any higher authority at the transnational level. State power to restrict them is not only confined to national boundaries, but is also constrained by the need of all states for the TNCs' participation in either disposing of surpluses or securing imports.

These TNCs cannot, therefore, be underestimated or ignored in the future, if any progress is to be made regarding world food management problems. What no analysis or policy proposal has taken account of is that these TNCs, to all intents and purposes, *are* the world grain trading system. Their power and scope of operations in it is such that in its present form, the world grain trading system would not function in their absence. But they will not disappear given that they constantly reinforce the structure of the system and hence their power within it, and because they are indispensable in that no alternative to them automatically presents itself. Whatever opinion is held about the efficacy of the service they provide, it is clear that the time has come to put these five TNCs at the forefront of analysis and policy-making regarding the world grain trading system.

Notes

1. Australian sorghum and Canadian rapeseed, unlike most other grains exported by these countries, are not marketed by government trading boards.
2. For a detailed study of the corporations' historical development, see Morgan (1979). Yet, as Morgan argues, a definitive history of the world grain trade has yet to be written.
3. An exception to this is the corporate ownership of land in Argentina and Brazil by Bunge and Born and, to a lesser extent, by Continental.
4. The transnationality of the trading operations of the corporations is illustrated by the following (albeit vastly over-simplified) example:

A cable arrives in New York, from one of Continental's overseas offices — say, Paris. A buyer has bid for 10,000 tons of soyabeans for July delivery in Rotterdam. Before accepting or countering with an offer, the trader considers future prices, world news, freight quotations, vessel bookings, the crop outlook, and the competition.

Then he makes a simple calculation. The basis for the final price is the quotation on the Chicago Board of Trade for July soyabeans. From that the trader subtracts the cost of buying the actual beans at, say, Seneca, Illinois. He adds in the barge freight to New Orleans, the cost of handling at Continental's elevator there, and the ocean freight to Rotterdam. Then he cables the Paris office with a cif price offer — cost, insurance and freight . . .

If he gets an 'accept' from the other side, he begins the ulcer-producing task of seeking out a profit of pennies or less per bushel. He tries to find cheap soyabeans, then he hedges his buying by selling July futures in Chicago. Since the futures price is the basis for his actual soyabean sale, he can limit losses this way. Or experience might tell him that the price of soyabeans will drop before he has to cover his sale. He may speculate on his hunch and wait to buy.

The chartering department, meanwhile, will be speculating on shipping, trying to get the best deal possible for the July delivery in Rotterdam. It may take a section of a ship under charter by another company. Or it may charter a tanker for the 10,000 sale; 30,000 excess may be filled by another sale, or it may figure on selling the space later to a competitor at a profit.

All these facts, and more, determine what Continental's profit on the sale will be. And, of course, whatever profit there is could be eroded if, for instance, the grain is late getting to New Orleans, delaying the ship's departure.

At any rate, it will be months before the trader will know if the sale to Rotterdam was a success. (*Business Week*, 11 March 1972.)

5. Gilmore (1982) has produced these and similar diagrams for all five companies.

6. There has been much speculation about the levels of profits the corporations achieved as a result of the great grain robbery. The companies go so far as to argue that they actually *lost* money on some of the transactions. Yet there is little doubt that net profits for the period were substantially above those of previous years. Whether these were the *direct* result of the sales to the Soviets, or the *indirect* result of the effects these sales had on the residual world market and grain prices, has more pertinence in an explicitly political or strategic context than in the more specific area of corporate development. A further point to remember is that private ownership of the corporations enables them to plough back a far higher proportion of profits into the company than would be possible with public stockholders.

References

Arroyo, G., 1979, *Bases Théoretiques et Méthodologiques d'un Projet*, Cahiers de Recherches 'Transnationales et Agriculture' no. 1, serie 1, CETRAL, Paris.

Bastin, G. and J. Ellis, 1980, *International Trade in Grains and the World Food Economy*, Economist Intelligence Unit, Special Report no 83, London.

Burbach, R. and P. Flynn, 1980, *Agribusiness in the Americas, Monthly Review Press* and NACLA, New York.

Business Week 11 March 1972, 'The Incredible Empire of Michel Fribourg'.

Business Week 16 April 1979, 'Cargill: Preparing for the Next Boom in Worldwide Trading'.

Debatisse, M., 1979, *Le Commerce International des Céréales*, Centre Français du Commerce Extérieur, Paris.

Gilmore, R., 1982, *A Poor Harvest: The Clash of Policies and Interests in the Grain Trade*, Longman, New York.

Goldberg, R., 1974, *Agribusiness Management for Developing Countries — Latin America*, Ballinger, Cambridge, Mass.

Grennes, T., P.R. Johnson·and M. Thursby, 1978, *The Economics of the World Grain Trade*, Praeger, New York.

Morgan, D., 1979, *Merchants of Grain*, Viking, New York.

Schmitz, A., A.F. McCalla, D.O. Mitchell and C. Carter, 1981, *Grain Export Cartels*, Ballinger, Cambridge, Mass.

Trager, J., 1975, *The Great Grain Robbery*, Ballantine Books, New York.

United States Senate Subcommittee on Multinational Corporations, 1976, *International Grain Companies*, Second Session, Hearings Before the Subcommittee on MNCs of the Committee on Foreign Relations, US Senate, 94th Congress, 18, 23 and 24 June, Part 16, US Government Printing Office, Washington DC (published 1977).

7 US-EUROPEAN AGRICULTURAL TRADE RELATIONS

Not for the first time agricultural trade has become a live and contentious issue in Atlantic relations. Questions of access and of protection have been subjects of constant concern to American farmers and traders since the establishment of Europe's Common Agricultural Policy. Now, though, under the pressures of surplus stocks of grain, and falling farm incomes, there is a new area of contention — competitive subsidies designed to win or secure shares in an erratic world market. Months of negotiation have failed to resolve the issue and neither the European Community nor the United States has shown any sign of being ready to sacrifice what both define as legitimate economic interests.

The bilateral relationship between the United States and the European Community has dominated international agricultural trade relations for the last thirty years. European and American attitudes to proposals for the liberalisation, regulation or management of key agricultural product markets have determined the role and success of international institutions, and the fate of attempts to reach international agreements on agricultural matters. Domestic policy decisions, taken in Brussels and Washington, have determined not only the state of the world market but have also become important and devisive items on the agenda of trade talks, ministerial meetings, and summits.

The attitudes and policies of the two sides have not remained constant throughout the period, and external circumstances as well as the dynamics of the domestic agricultural policies pursued on each side of the Atlantic have shifted the areas of contention. The issues at stake in the current set of bilateral negotiations — initiated after the ministerial meeting of GATT (the General Agreement on Tariffs and Trade) in November 1982 had failed to make any significant progress on agricultural trade matters — are very different from those of a decade or two decades ago.

In the early rounds of GATT negotiations in the late 1940s and early 1950s, agriculture was not a central issue. Only 15 per cent of international grain production was traded in 1950. The individual countries which were to become the member states of the European

Community pursued generally protectionist policies but limited technology left them with a significant import requirement — sufficient to satisfy the export capabilities of the North American wheat and corn producers. In the United States less than 20 per cent of grain production went for export; exports were always important but had little of the crucial significance they have acquired over the last two decades.

In the early 1950s the central concern of the US agricultural community was to preserve and protect agricultural development and the often hard-pressed American farmer from foreign trade. For years the US Administration dragged its feet in the face of attempts by GATT and exporting countries such as Australia to liberalise agricultural trade. As a recent study concluded, 'The US found itself having to defend its disruptive actions on agricultural import restrictions, disposal of surplus stocks and use of export subsidies'[1] — all elements of an agricultural policy tailored to domestic farm prices and farm income support, not to trade expansion. In 1955 after several years during which the US had been in violation of its GATT obligations because of its domestic policies, the Eisenhower administration was finally granted a formal waiver. Direct support of the US farm sector, under legislation dating back to the 1930s was made legal, but the opportunity of including agriculture with the other industries covered by the various GATT agreements was lost. The American action confirmed the view that agricultural policy was a matter for domestic decision, not international agreement.

Although the problem of surplus grain was emerging, and export trade growing, the balance of interests within the US farm sector was still firmly on the side of those seeking protection.

The balance of American opinion changed as the Common Agricultural Policy of the newly formed European Economic Community began to emerge after 1957. American negotiators entered the Kennedy Round trade talks of the 1960s with a nominal commitment to inclusion of agriculture alongside trade in manufactured goods in the GATT agreements, but there remained a degree of ambivalence at the heart of the American position. On the one hand American producers saw the Europeans institutionalising measures to protect national markets which their own exports would have difficulty in penetrating. The need for secure and growing commercial exports was increasing, especially for US grain, the output of which grew by 25 per cent between 1950 and

1960. From 1954 on the Eisenhower Administration initiated and steadily expanded the PL480 programme which distributed surplus grain on concessional terms to less-developed countries. Though productivity spurred on by technical advance was expanding at unprecedented rates, US farmers were still suffering declining real incomes and were falling further behind their counterparts in industry.

That, though, would be an incomplete picture to present. Other US farmers feared liberalisation of trade since it posed a direct threat to their own livelihoods. The CAP as set out in the 1958 Stresa conference was by no means the rapacious monster which in US mythology it has since become. 'Compared with the widespread use of quantitative trade restrictions in national policies the basic instruments of the CAP looked rather liberal.'[2] Price levels were not fixed, leaving open the prospect that traditional US markets would not be disturbed. There was some emphasis on structural policy which it was thought would reduce both the number of farmers and potential output given the right set of support prices. German interests were thought likely to balance out the inevitable pressure from the French for a strongly protectionist agricultural system.

It was only over time that the highly protectionist nature of the CAP became apparent, in particular its use of the system of variable import levies designed to insulate domestic producers from any fluctuations on world markets and its very high basic support prices established to keep the most marginal producer in business. There were also political factors which softened the US response to the Common Agricultural Policy. The establishment of the EEC and the wider ideal of European cooperation were central to US foreign policy objectives, which more than outweighed parochial agricultural concerns. The true difficulties which the nature of the CAP, and the method of operation of its mechanisms were going to present to the USA only emerged later.

Within the Community external protests from America and elsewhere were considered to be a marginal concern. The Community members were still large-scale importers of US grain, were running a substantial deficit with the USA on agriculture trade as a whole, and did not take seriously the possibility that the dynamic effects of the CAP on the European farm sector would radically alter that situation. Disputes such as the chicken war in 1962–3 when the substitution of high CAP levies for the lower German tariffs which had existed previously on poultry imports cut the USA out of the market, were treated as minor squabbles. Once the mechanisms of the CAP had been agreed the EEC had difficulty in responding to international challenges. The CAP was not only a major achievement of common action but also part of 'an internal bargain, compensating agricultural exporters among member countries for the improved access to their non-agricultural markets which more-industrialised countries had gained'.[3]

It was in this context that the Community offered its major concession on the CAP in response to the rising volume of US protest in the early months of the Kennedy Round negotiations. Few Europeans took seriously American calls for fully open access, or for the exposure of agricultural trade practices to the full scrutiny of GATT. American attempts to have levies converted to fixed tariffs, with the aim of reducing and eliminating those tariffs by the same percentage reductions applied to industrial trade, were regarded as naive. US hopes of forcing the Europeans to shift the basis of farm support to income supplements, and away from guaranteed prices which acted as incentives to production were regarded as undue external interference in the domestic affairs of the Community, as well as hypocritical, given the failure of the US government to carry through a similar programme at home.

Instead the Community proposed what it regarded as a practical and political realistic solution to the dispute, a *montant de soutien* — a freezing of all forms of support to producers of particular products, including grains. For the Community the offer was a genuine concession — in that it placed a restriction on measures considered to be essentially matters of internal policy; and at the same time a negotiating device — in that it established the CAP as an accepted and legitimised part of the international trading structure.

The proposal was that the agricultural part of the Kennedy Round negotiations should aim at consoliating all measures of support for agriculture whatever their form with an agreement that a ceiling of the total level of support would not be breached. The objective was neither harmonisation nor the removal of subsidies but the limitation of their growth.

To the USA the proposal became acceptable only in retrospect as the consequences of the CAP on production and trade became obvious. At the time it was seen as an entrenchment of protectionist domestic policies and a step away from, rather than towards, liberalisation or open access. The USA sought instead guarantees of access for particular products, including most prominently confirmation that soyabeans would not be liable to import tariffs in line with an agreement originally reached during the Dillon Round of GATT talks.

Eventually in order to avoid the breakdown of the overall trade talks the EEC accepted bilateral arrangements with the USA which granted a number of specific tariff and access concessions on priority products. The grain negotiations were transferred from the Kennedy Round negotiations to the International Wheat Council's discussions on an international grains agreement.

Under the pressure of falling world prices attempts to set an agreed floor price and to determine market shares for the main exporting countries proved unsustainable, even though an initial grains agreement was negotiated and ratified. Disputes over the pricing formula led to a breakdown in discussions and a reversion to the well-established pattern of imperfect competition. The only economic provision of the Grains Agreement which survived was a limited convention on Food Aid. The failure of the rest of the Agreement, after almost a decade of talks reinforced the view that grain and agricultural trade in general were immune to the application of international management.

It can be argued that by the early 1970s the USA had adjusted to the CAP even though it maintained, in common with other exporters, a rhetorical commitment to open access and liberalisation. The USA had begun to find new and highly lucrative markets in the Community. Exports to the EEC of soyabeans, free of duty, had expanded by 50 per cent in the decade up to 1970. Agricultural exports to the Community were higher than ever before and with soyabeans in particular the USA had found a trade which the CAP, by pricing Europe's indigenous grain at a high level even to its own livestock producers, actually encouraged. EEC support for meat production also encouraged an expansion of European livestock, which while a source of dismay for the Australians and other meat traders, ensured a stable and growing market for animal feed.

American concern at the absorption of the British market by the Community after 1973 and fears that Australia's and New Zealand's trade would be redirected from Britain to other markets was mitigated for a time by the belief that British accession would lead to a fundamental alteration of the CAP, or at the least to an adjustment of common price levels downwards — a belief justified not least by the commitments of British politicians.

American agricultural exports began to expand rapidly. Enlargement of the world market by Soviet purchases and by the growth of trade with Japan and the developing countries of South East Asia in the prosperous days of the early 1970s pushed exports of wheat as a proportion of US production up to 76.8 per cent in 1972. One observer commented that the circumstances of the early 1970s — disappearance of stocks, rising Third World demand and growing Soviet imports — offered the possibility that the climacteric was past. That perception was not of course shared by all. For parts of the farming industry the development of the CAP and the extension of European self-sufficiency undermined previously secure markets. Therefore although the Tokyo Declaration of 1973, the statement of intent opening the trade negotiations, made clear the common acceptance of the special status of agriculture, the USA retained the hope that external and internal pressures would force change upon the CAP.

The target for the US negotiators was the widespread use of export subsidies and other non-tariff barriers. The twin aims were to secure existing agreements on access (particularly that relating to soyabeans) and to ensure that the output trends of the farm sector under the CAP did not threaten US markets elsewhere. Behind the US stance there was emerging 'a changed attitude to export markets — markets which could no longer be taken for granted and were no longer simply dumping grounds.'[4]

The European position was stated in the Council of Ministers Mandate for the Tokyo Round:

> The specific objective of the agricultural negotiations should be the expansion of trade in stable world markets, in accordance with existing agricultural policies . . . by means of appropriate international agreements.

The European approach to the problems of agricultural trade was one of international management in the interests of supply security and price stability within a limited range for markets which were proving to be insecure and volatile. The Community emphasised the disruptive effect of the US soyabean embargo in 1973 as an example of the instability which agreement on security of supply could mitigate. EEC representatives argued for some form of stock holding as a means of underpinning the market and the isolation of agriculture as a separate subject of negotiation, clearly distinct from the wider discussions of trade policy in the Tokyo Round.

In contrast to the US desire to meet the problem of instability and world food shortage by making the market mechanism work more effectively, the Community favoured international trade management — a reflection of its own internal approach to agricultural policy.

From the beginning the Community argued in the words of the Mandate that 'the CAP's principles and mechanisms should not be called into question and do not constitute a matter for negotiation' — a point which the USA had come to accept as far as the internal workings of the CAP were concerned, though not of course in respect of its external effects. Neither the US characterisation of the CAP as 'the ultimate in mercantilism' nor the European concern with world food security can be taken entirely at face value. The divergent approaches owed more to immediate interests than to any ideological conflict. The best way to assist US exports was undoubtedly to argue for the abandonment of trade restrictions by importers while for the EEC any argument which shielded domestic market management against external pressures was to be embraced.

The latest round of negotiations which opened in December 1982 has been made necessary by the inadequacies of the Tokyo Round and the vagueness of the agreements signed by both sides in an effort to bring the trade talks to a close after six years of discussion. For two of those years the failure to resolve differences of opinion on how agricultural trade problems should be handled meant that the negotiations were more or less stalled. The eventual resolution owed more to exhaustion than to genuine agreement. It left the EEC able to claim that its long-term aim of 'legalizing the CAP' had been achieved and the USA confident that the clauses of the agreement relating to export subsidies would limit the freedom of action of the EEC in attempting to win new markets. The American hope was that this would force the EEC to reform itself as financial pressures became the dominant factor in the calculation. That long-standing US aspiration has yet to be fulfilled.

The key to the Tokyo Round settlement and to the present disputes lies in the clause of the 1979 agreement which refers to export subsidies. That clause binds signatories 'not to grant directly or indirectly any export subsidy on certain primary products in a manner which results in the signatory granting such subsidy having more than an equitable share of world export trade in such product, account being taken of the shares of the signatories in trade in the product concerned during a previous representative period, and any special factors which may have affected or may be affecting trade in such product.' More than an equitable share of world export trade is defined to include 'any case in which the effect of an export subsidy granted by a signatory is to displace the exports of another signatory bearing in mind the developments on world markets.'

Although the intention of the clause may appear clear, much scope for disagreement remains. The Community has always regarded export restitutions[5] as an integral part of its domestic agricultural policy. The fact that they enable European farm produce to be sold at or below world market prices, and that traders can rely on the availability of credit, often on terms very favourable to the importing countries, does not in the EEC view constitute a particularly aggressive trading policy but rather normal commercial practice, simply matching the export promotion of other countries, including of course the USA. The Community is under constant pressure from those member states with strong agricultural sectors, particularly France, and from the agricultural lobby generally, to develop an explicit export policy.

The demand for a sustained export strategy has grown stronger as the problems of surplus disposal have increased. The French view has been expressed by Henri Nouyrit, the Deputy Director of the French Confederation of Agricultural Cooperatives:

> For exports there is no real policy. So called 'surpluses' are disposed of as the opportunity arises. There is no plan for exports, no medium term policy. Exports have become a sort of undesirable adjunct to intervention. Financial pre-occupations over export restitutions have inhibited a proper commercial policy involving an effort to establish permanent trade flows, to seek out new markets and to develop commercial instruments such as credits and long term contracts.[6]

To an extent the Commission has shifted towards the French position. The notion of long-term contracts and special credit facilities has been floated on a number of occasions and the Commission's *Reflections on the CAP* published in 1981 talked openly of pursuing the success of its exports in coming years, 'by providing the CAP with instruments similar to those enjoyed by major agricultural exporting countries (the United States, Canada, Australia and New Zealand), in particular the ability to conclude long term agreements.'

Since then, although Britain and West Germany are reported to be less than fully convinced, the Commission has 'coalesced around the proposition that the Community should at least have the instrument (in Community jargon, "framework agreements for multiannual supply") available.'[7] The idea has been raised again in the discussion paper presented by the Farm Commissioner, Dr Andriessen, to European agriculture ministers on 28 May 1985. The paper proposed among a list of other initiatives 'a fresh look at trade mechanisms to allow EEC exporters the use of export credits, long term supply agreements and links between commercial exports and food aid.'[8]

The paper along with the subsequent formal Commission documents on the future of the CAP sets these proposals in the context of a renegotiation of GATT with some parallel liberalisation of agricultural imports into the Community being necessary to buy off US and other opposition.

In the United States both officials and commentators believed that the Tokyo Round settlement in 1979 marked a firm agreement, with the internal arrangements of the CAP accepted, but the role of subsidised European output on world markets firmly restricted. Their disillusionment explains some of the anger which has crept into the current dispute.

World market conditions have given the argument its new sense of urgency. Since 1980, despite exceptionally large-scale Soviet imports, and the development of a new market in China, world prices for grain have continued to fall and stocks, held involuntarily, have continued to accumulate. The US farmer-owned reserve, a temporary stock holding measure when it was introduced in 1977, expanded remorselessly. US yields, productivity and total output have continued to grow but the shortfall of effective demand, in what has become a buyers' market, has both pushed up the cost of government support and left farm income falling.

It is not surprising that the mood of farmers and traders alike is gloomy. In the words of Ted Halow, the executive director of the North American Grain Exporters Association, 'The world grain trade is shrinking, the 1970s are behind us, the period of rapid grain expansion is behind us . . . probably forever.'

It is understandable given this mood that the United States should have reacted so strongly to the European interpretation of the Tokyo Round agreement and to the drift of European policy. Since the Tokyo Round agreement was signed in 1979 European exports of wheat have risen by over 100 per cent. European production has grown while consumption is barely rising, generating an increasing surplus volume for export. Though the EEC export trade is still small by American standards, every ton has become a subject of controversy given the condition of the market. Ted Halow's comment that 'European farmers are producing not for consumers but for intervention' is difficult to refute. The degree of farm support has been the subject of sustained statistical dispute. While the EEC prefers to talk in terms of support per farmer, since that is the measure which favours its conclusion that European support levels are reasonable and fair, the USA with larger farms quotes figures on support for each unit of output. The numbers game apart, however, the basic position is not in dispute.

Clearly the absolute level of European support, plus the security of income for each unit of production without limit, has induced added production. Saturation of demand at current price levels has created surpluses which depress world market prices and require disposal. The system of export restitutions has allowed European farmers to export at world market prices — prices which their own production costs could not sustain. The effect of this is not of course limited to the grain market. In 1974 the Community was a major importer of dairy products, sugar and beef. By 1981 it had become the world's largest dairy exporter, number two in world sugar trade and the exporter of over 60,000 tons of beef.

The United States too has supported its producers, though the level of support per unit of output is lower and the blanket guarantee of income given to the European farmers is absent.

US production costs are undoubtedly lower, and on economic criteria of comparative advantage the US case is strong. Such criteria, however, are unlikely to form the basis of any settlement of the current dispute. There may be much justice on the side of the United States but the complications of the US-European relationship in agricultural matters and beyond will make a resolution favourable to the USA more difficult to achieve than the administration may imagine.

For the last three years the dispute has been conducted through rhetoric. Mr Seeley Lodwic, the US Assistant Secretary for Agriculture, described the European strategy as 'targeting key US markets

. . . seeking to shift the cost of domestic programmes to other trading countries through unfair competition.' Mr Turner Oyloe, the US agricultural attaché in London, speaking to the Oxford Farm Conference, argued that if the CAP were carried to its logical conclusion, 'greenhouses should be installed in Ireland to grow oranges, bananas and coffee'. John Block, the US agriculture secretary accused the EEC of 'literally stealing markets away from the US, Canada, Australia, the developing countries and others in sugar, poultry and wheat'. He was later reported to be pressing President Reagan 'to fight fire with fire'.

The aggressive response from the European side has come mainly from the French. Even as the discussions set up after the GATT ministerial meeting were getting under way Mme. Edith Cresson, then the French Agriculture Minister, accused the United States of 'exporting its economic crisis' and said that its new farm policies were 'motivated by domestic political concerns'. The Commission itself has been less strident but equally unyielding. Its annual review of the agricultural situation in the Community published at the end of 1982 says:

> The Community's relations with its GATT partners in so far as agriculture is concerned were marked by an intensification of the attacks on the CAP. Certain agricultural exporters — in particular the United States — invoked GATT dispute settlement procedures to pillory various aspects of the Common Agricultural Policy . . . The Community reacted to these attacks with moderation, and a determination to show that it complied scrupulously with GATT rules.

The rhetoric has been interspersed with brief periods during which it appeared that an amicable resolution was being sought through negotiations. In advance of the November 1982 GATT meeting Block emphasised the limited nature of the US challenge: 'We don't challenge the CAP — but we do challenge the export subsidies that make it difficult if not impossible to compete'. Block was reported as declaring that there would be 'no trade war' and the agreement to initiate bilateral discussions after the Geneva ministerial meeting appeared to confirm the view.

For a brief period the USA appeared to be seeking ways to limit production as its way out of the twin problems of surplus stocks and low income. The Payment in Kind scheme, through which the administration hoped both to reduce stocks and to cut production by inducing farmers to leave up to 25 per cent of their land unplanted was pursued by President Reagan despite an initial failure to win formal Congressional support. The scheme was reported to be considered 'a supply side solution' by the administration and an indication that 'the President and the Secretary of Agriculture have apparently abandoned hope that export expansion and large scale sales to the Soviets will absorb the huge American grain surplus'.[9]

It soon became clear, however, that the Payment in Kind scheme was not a complete solution, and that there were many in the US Administration unwilling to see US agriculture absorb all the costs of what they regarded with some justice as unfair European competition. The effect of a 25 per cent cutback in production if sustained over several years on local business in the affected areas and on those major companies whose survival depends on sales of farm equipment, machinery and fertiliser would have been harsh. From the farmers' point of view the scheme offered no major cut in overheads, nor any promise of increased income and the incentive was for each individual to maximise the benefit to himself by leaving his least productive fields unplanted and by raising the yield from the rest. Stocks did fall but neither that effect nor the impact of the Payment in Kind programme on prices was permanent. Instead the USA found other producers eagerly adding to their shares in the world market. The irony of the fact that a major beneficiary of the temporary rise in prices and the improved export opportunities was the CAP has not been lost.

As the debate on Payment in Kind proceeded the advocates of a firm policy against the European Community gathered strength, and support. At the beginning of December 1982 Richard Lyng the Deputy Agriculture Secretary was reported as saying that the USDA was 'preparing a plan and package in response to the European stance on agricultural subsidies — updating its list of US exports which might be subsidised — chickens, eggs, raisins, wheat flour and pasta'. Proposals were put forward for extending the Payment in Kind scheme to exports — granting purchasers additional supplies from existing stocks at discount rates. Senator Jesse Helms supporting the proposal told the Senate agriculture committee that 'the EEC's right to swing their export subsidy fist ends at Uncle Sam's nose'. President Reagan in a speech to the American Farm Bureau Federation announced that he was extending the export credit programme by 50 per cent 'to help counter the massive European subsidies and eventually to bring an end to such practices'.

The decision to subsidise the sale of 1 million tons of wheat flour to Egypt came as the unsurprising conclusion to a long period of verbal exchanges. Sales of subsidised butter to Egypt are reported to be under consideration, and negotiations on the possibilities for subsidised sales of wheat, maize and other products to eleven markets began. They included at least five — Portugal, Yugoslavia, Morocco, Pakistan and Yemen, as well as Egypt — which are considered traditional EEC outlets. Then after a further year of desultory negotiations, and the virtual abandonment of the PIK programme as a strategy the second Reagan Administration introduced a new and more aggressive programme to support exports which adds bonuses from government stocks to otherwise commercial deals. The first use of the programme came in May 1985 with a deal involving grain sales to Algeria. With a two billion dollar budget the bonus scheme now appears to be an entrenched part of US Government agricultural policy. What remains unclear, however, is the nature of the US strategy and the extent to which it can overcome the weaknesses in the US position.

Leaving aside the legality of American action under GATT rules, a matter which is now the subject of an EEC challenge,[10] a strategy of sustained subsidy of exports raises a number of problems and leaves untouched the key political issue for the US Administration — low farm incomes and the accelerating rate of farm bankruptcies.

Taken individually the use of bonuses from stocks and other measures of subsidy are, of course, well within the means of the US Government. However, disposal of even 10 or 20 million tons of the current stocks of over 100 million tons will begin to pose a significant burden. That cost will rise if the Community responds as it began to after the Egyptian sale with matching subsidies. Then the Community agreed to a subsidy of £1.6 million for flour sales to Egypt and gave a special rebate to the Chinese in order to secure a sale of 600,000 tons of wheat.[11]

Unless bonuses and subsidies are able to win a significant additional share of the world market for the United States, there would also be balance of payments costs from falling real prices. Given the Community's current pricing policy, and the smaller volume involved, the additional input of Community resources required to match US subsidies would be rather small. The cost to both sides would of course increase if the conflict spread to other agricultural products in the dairy sector or elsewhere.

It is the prospect of a lower world price which poses the most serious problem for the advocates of an all-out US export subsidy strategy. Unless production is adjusted downwards (a slow and difficult process given the limitations of the price transmission mechanisms and the strength of national policies) any price fall would clearly damage the interests of US farmers and traders who rely on world market prices. The prospect of a spiral of subsidy and falling prices must be a cause of considerable concern to an administration with a budget deficit of $200 billion and a hostile farm sector whose incomes have fallen by as much as 20 per cent in three years, and whose lobby groups are now calling on the administration not simply to challenge the CAP but to create a structure of agricultural support in the USA along the lines of that in Europe. The effect of a strong dollar on the competitiveness of US agriculture is adding to that pressure.

It is also clear that some of these potential costs are well perceived by the administration and that the subsidy of the sale to Algeria, as to Egypt in 1983, may represent a 'warning shot' designed to make the European Community reconsider its policies rather than the beginning of a long-term subsidy policy, or part of a well-planned trade offensive.

The nature of the possible European response, however, may not have been assessed in full. In agricultural trade as a whole the US has a net surplus with the Community of some $6 billion per year ($7 billion in 1981). Soyabean sales alone have sustained and indeed improved the USA's net trade balance with the Community. Current US action risks retaliation which may well add the cost of lost European markets to the cost of subsidies.

The fact that half of the USA's agricultural exports to the EEC enter the Community duty free has already been noted by the French who have proposed a ceiling on soyabean imports which are immune from import levies under agreements signed 25 years ago, and which have risen four-fold in volume since then. To the Community as a whole the imposition of such a levy against past undertakings would be a measure of last resort, or as one commentator put it, 'an ultimate deterrent'. By March 1984 the EEC Foreign Ministers were ordering the preparation of regulations setting import limits on cereal substitutes, including corn gluten feed.[12]

In the studiously vague prose of the Commission's *Reflections on the CAP*:

> The Commission will continue to honour its obligations including those contracted in international organizations but at a time when new restraints must be imposed there must be more vigilance over the import of certain feeding stuffs and similar products. These measures would help to arrest the excessive rise in imports of these substitutes.

In the medium term a further response would be the use by the Community of its control over the price mechanism in order to reduce consumption of imported products, such as soyabeans, by providing some inducement to European animal feed producers to use some of the current EEC surplus supplies of grain — at present priced out of the market. In April 1983 Poul Dalsager, then the EEC's agriculture commissioner, announced plans to make two to three million tons of surplus cereals available for feeding to livestock at subsidised prices.[13] There is speculation that the scale of the initiative will be extended as soon as the Community's budget crisis is resolved and the issue is revived in the recent Commission document on the future of the CAP, the Perspectives paper issued in June 1985.[14] A mixture of the two proposals — a levy on imported animal feed imports, the proceeds of which would support the use of home grown grain — would reduce the costs and also reduce the volume of surplus grain to be exported (therefore also reducing the burden of export restitutions required). The cost to the Community would depend upon the level of duty set, and the degree of subsidy to animal feed producers to meet all or part of the difference between the cost of current imports and the cost of Community produce. To reluctant governments within the Community the approach might be presented as a means both of securing the CAP — an important symbol of the Community's existence for all its faults — and of averting a trade war of export subsidies by diverting some currently exported grain back into the Community itself.

There are many possible variations on the scheme, including a volume limit on soyabean imports (with or without a levy). They would all cost the Americans their growing market in the Community and a part of their positive trade balance with Europe. Although current European export markets might be reduced or held static as grain was diverted to internal use, the gain for US exporters would be matched by the burden of unsold soyabean crops.

After years of negotiation and of warning shots and legal challenges from both sides of the Atlantic it is difficult to conclude that a resolution is imminent. On the American side the hope persists that the EEC's budget problems will force a radical change of policy in relation to agriculture. To the European side American plans — in relation to export subsidies and the Payment in Kind scheme — appear ill-defined and uncertain. Both sides harbour the hope that a sudden world shortage of grain will solve the problem, and avert the need to put on the negotiating table the domestic agricultural policies which have created the current difficulties.

All seem to be false hopes. The EEC has made repeated assertions of its wish to bring its own prices into line with those prevailing on world markets, but the speed of change has been very slow, and productivity growth has outstripped the very small decline in real prices with the result that output has continued to rise. The EEC budget ceiling has posed a problem for the ten member states but the agreement on increased contribution levels reached in 1984 and confirmed after the settlement of negotiations on Community enlargement in 1985 remove the problem for the moment. The accession of Spain and Portugal, coupled with new Community programmes for regional and Soviet policy may put new strains even on the increased budget before the end of the 1980s but the events of 1984 and 1985 have shown that in the last resort political commitment to the EEC can overcome even the most serious concerns about agricultural spending.

Equally it seems unrealistic for Europeans to assume that the US Government will absorb all the costs of the downturn in world markets. The fact that under the Payment in Kind scheme the USA paid its farmers not to produce while output from Canada, Argentina and the EEC was increasing did not go unnoticed. Many in the Reagan Administration are undoubtedly happier pursuing an aggressive export policy to restore the US position in world markets instead of making such payments, or seeking a new grains sales agreement with the Soviet Union from the position of supplicant.

Neither side can seriously expect world market conditions to solve the problem for them. Stocks, according to the International Wheat Council,[15] are now running at over 270 million metric tons and for the year ahead the chances are of increased output in the Soviet Union, Australia, Argentina and other producing countries.

For the moment it may well be that diplomatic concerns take precedence over agricultural issues and that the grain dispute is subsumed as debate inside the alliance concentrates on crucial political and strategic matters, in particular the issue of arms control and the Strategic Defence Initiative. But the removal of agricultural disputes from the headlines to, say, a bilateral committee charged to research and report, should not be mistaken for a solution. Agricultural trade will return to the agenda again and again until a solution of some permanence is found. Conflict over grain and other agricultural products, particularly dairy produce, will reassert itself even if a temporary ceasefire is pasted together.

Can an acceptable and lasting solution be found? For all the immediate difficulties I believe that the answer is yes. There are many in the EEC who seek a more rational agricultural structure, and who do not wish to see the Community become simply a Farmers' Union. In the United States farm spending is already casting a long, and unwanted shadow over the Federal budget.

The long-term solution to the common problem lies in a joint agreement on the reduction of subsidies. The USA has already frozen its dairy support levels for four years, and is now proposing the freezing of target prices for grains. The EEC began by making gentle cuts through a formula which cuts prices by 1 per cent for every 1 million tons of production over and above planned levels. Greater reductions, in nominal as well as real terms, will be necessary to reduce output given the pressures of technological advance. A programme of such cuts, with agreed production targets, should be the aim. So too should a strict ceiling on export subsidies, in order to prevent the disruption of the world market and for the purpose of avoiding the gross misallocation of resources which subsidies involve. Over any interim period some temporary agreement on the allocation of markets may be necessary though a full-blown, formal agreement is probably unattainable as well as undesirable.[16]

There would be no one clear winner from such a solution. The US would retain its world markets so long as it could compete with Argentina, Canada and other producers on price and on the security of its supplies. In the EEC grain production would plateau and lower grain prices might stimulate the use of grain by the neglected indigenous livestock sector. On both sides the direct costs of subsidies and restitutions would be reduced, freeing resources for alternative investment in other agricultural sectors, or in other parts of the rural economy.

Though the importing countries of the world undoubtedly benefit from the subsidies poured into agriculture by the exporters, cheap grain imports have proved a disincentive to the development of production. Given the appropriate response the reduction of subsidies would have beneficial effects here too.

A move towards such a solution would require from both the European Community and the United States something more than consent to particular sets of figures and timetables. It would mark a willingness to see agricultural policy in international and not strictly national terms, and a change of direction against the trend in so many other sectors. There is sadly no sign as yet that any such willingness exists at the political level.

More likely for the foreseeable future is a continuing conflict, with sporadic outbreaks of hostilities. Leaving aside the waste of resources which that implies, the chief concern must be that agricultural disputes, after arguments over steel and the question of East–West trade, will contribute to the undermining of the cooperative trading relationship built up over the last four decades. In trade matters Europe and America are already beginning to look less like partners and more like adversaries. In the words of the former French Agriculture Minister Michel Rocard: 'trading relations between the US and Europe are characterized by bad faith, lack of trust and harmful, simplistic and over harsh criticism'.[17] Disputes over the last few years have had a corrosive effect on the trust which should form the basis of the alliance. Further disputes, whether conducted through rhetoric, selective statistics, or open measures of economic warfare will do nothing to repair the damage.

Notes

1. T.K. Warley, *International Economic Relations of the Western World,* Vol. 1, Part 3, Royal Institute of International Affairs, 1976.

2. S. Tangermann, 'Agricultural Trade Relations between the European Community and Temperate Food Exporting Countries', *European Review of Agricultural Economics,* 1979.

3. Ibid.

4. J. Hillman, 'Policy Issues Relevant to US Agricultural Trade' in A.F. McCalla and T.E. Josling, *Imperfect Markets in Agricultural Trade,* Allanhead Osmun, 1981.

5. Export restitutions are payments to producers which allow them to compete on the world market. They have accounted for 45–50 per cent of the total EEC farm budget in the first half of the 1980s.

6. H. Nouyrit, 'Perspectives de développement des principes productions

agricoles françaises en relation avec le Marché mondial; Remarques sur l'aide alimentaire' in M. Tracey and I. Hodac, *Prospects for Agriculture in the European Community*, College of Europe, Bruges, 1979.

7. *Financial Times*, 9 August 1982.

8. *Financial Times*, 29 May 1982.

9. *Financial Times*, 6 January 1983.

10. *Financial Times*, 24 May 1985.

11. *The Times*, 27 October 1983.

12. *World Commodity Report, Financial Times*, 14 March 1984..

13. *Financial Times*, 21 April 1983.

14. *Financial Times*, 2 July 1985. The paper also raises the possibility of using grain to produce ethanol.

15. International Wheat Council, *Market Report*, July 1985.

16. The EEC has recently reasserted this idea but the proposal from M. Claude Villain, the European Commission's Director General for Agriculture was immediately rejected by US officials — *Financial Times*, 7 April 1984. The proposal was rejected by President Mitterrand addressing the World Food Council in June 1985 — *Financial Times*, 11 June 1985.

17. *Wall Street Journal*, 25 April 1984.

8 PROSPECTS FOR THE WORLD GRAIN TRADE: THE CHINESE MARKET

Of all the countries considered here the one which by its own decisions could have the most influence in altering the shape of the grain market over the next two decades is China. With a population of a billion and a quarter or more by the end of the century, a decision to import on a major scale and to satisfy even a proportion of the potential demand for meat and improved diets which now exists would transform the world market. Equally, a reversion to self-sufficiency balancing wheat imports with limited exports of surplus rice and thereby avoiding additional pressures on the balance of payments would sharply diminish the role of the world's second largest purchaser of grain.

No calculation can provide an accurate prediction of what will in the end be a political decision. Current trends suggest that net grain imports on a significant scale are being incorporated into national planning for the next decade. At the same time, however, the detail of policy indicates that there remains in the modernisation process an element of caution, and a determination to avoid dependence on external sources even more distinct than in the Soviet Union.

The last thirty-five years have seen remarkable achievements in Chinese agriculture and in the food supply system. Although almost all the statistics are speculative, and the subject of constant reinterpretation[1] the general position is not disputed. Agricultural output has risen by some 3 per cent per annum since the early 1950s, and output of grain, including rice, by over 350 per cent. The gross inadequacies and irregularities of food supply which characterised the pre-revolutionary period have been substantially eliminated. Production, though still predominantly labour-intensive, has been supported by the gradual introduction of new technology and by the development and use of higher yielding seeds, and fertilisers. The distribution of food has been much improved, through rationing, and there is a measure of equality in consumption levels between regions, unprecedented before 1949. China's achievement in yields and in the provision of food on an even per capita basis exceed those of most developing countries. As Peter Timmer has written, the extent of historic production success and of future production problems are summed up by a simple comparison of Chinese and Indian agricultural performance. In 1980 China produced a quarter more grain per capita, for half again as many people, from three quarters of the arable land.[2] Table 8.1 shows the pattern of grain production in China since 1949.

The achievement has been far from effortless and in particular competition for the resources necessary to sustain the growth of output has always been strong. In the mid to late 1950s the political priority given to industry, as the emphasis of economic development was placed on the mass mobilisation of labour, meant that investment in agriculture declined. Stark shortages of supply in the early 1960s led to a partial reversal of the policy and to the recognition that agriculture remained not only the major employment sector, but also a vital national resource, its importance re-emphasised by China's political isolation. From then on, though more explicitly in the 1970s, China has pursued a more clearly defined 'agriculture-first' strategy even though competing claims — for social, industrial, energy and military expenditure — have remained strong.

On the demand side the most significant factor has been the remorseless growth of population which on the World Bank's estimate has risen from 600 million to 1,019 million in the period between the mid-1950s and 1983.[3] Population growth, though it has slowed from the 1960s rate of 2.4 per cent per annum to some 1.2 per cent in response to government exhortations and incentives, continues to add some 12 million to the total each year. Improvements in nutrition have, of course, contributed to the growth.

Table 8.1:　China: Grain Production (million metric tons)

	Wheat	Rice	Feedgrains	Total grain
1949	14	49	13	110
1960	22	78	19	171
1970	31	102	29	240
1980	54	139	61	320
1982	68	161	85	355
1983	81	169	92	387
1984	88	178	95	407

Note: Total grain figures, in line with Chinese conventions, include potatoes.
Source: International Wheat Council, *World Wheat Situation*, various issues and FAO production yearbooks.

The result has been that despite the expansion of output of basic agricultural commodities, per capita consumption remains at the level of the 1950s, at around 280 kilograms per day. Though it is spread more evenly by the rationing system, differences between production in different areas are reflected to a degree in consumption patterns.[4] In the South and in much of the rural part of the country rice is still the stable component of the diet. Rice continues to provide 40 per cent of the country's total grain production. By contrast wheat has become the staple food of Northern China, including the principal industrial areas. The other grains produced, including maize and barley, are also used predominantly for human consumption with millet and some barley devoted to animal feed. The differences go beyond this simple distinction and there are inequities not just in the composition but also in the quality and quantity of food consumed. Regional disparities, in particular the low levels of consumption in areas where consumers for geographic or climatic reasons are unable to maintain self-sufficiency are still considered a major problem. Urbanisation as well as the maintenance of a large permanent army on the Northern border, has increased the requirement placed upon the communes, the basic unit of agricultural organisation, to provide grain to central government.

The problems of managing the internal distribution of grain from the major producing areas have at times been serious and in the words of the International Wheat Council it has proved simpler and cheaper to import grain to meet requirements in the heavily populated coastal areas. This pattern of supply has meant that import trends in the recent past have not reacted to fluctuations in domestic output and have remained high despite the growth of indigenous production. Despite these caveats, the record of agricultural progress remains remarkable, all the more so because for a decade development was constrained by the distractions of the Cultural Revolution. The adaptation of new farm management techniques, the growth of scientific research, and the introduction of more modern technology were all delayed as they became the subject of often bitter public controversy. Only in the changed atmosphere after 1976 did a full and open debate on the country's agricultural needs and the means of achievement become possible.

The agricultural policies adopted at the 1978 Communist Party Congress have sustained development and regenerated the growth of production which had slowed down during the years of the

Cultural Revolution. Yields, measured in terms of quintals per hectare, have risen by 22 per cent since 1978 with production of both rice and wheat significantly improved. Total grain production in the 1984 crop year was some 407 million metric tons, an increase of 42 per cent on 1978, according to IWC estimates.[5]

The main feature of the reforms adopted at the 1978 Party Congress and elaborated since, was the creation of a system of 'responsibility' under which income is determined by output and where the family is the basic unit of production. Land is now assigned to households on contracts which specify fixed production quotas. Above and beyond those quotas, production will be available for sale by the family through markets — providing additional income on the basis of productivity. Private plots as such are also being encouraged and in recent months the geographical range of private sales has been widened having previously been narrowly confined to a small local area.

Though the communes, which formed the basis of the old system, have not been abolished, the introduction of a major element of private trade stands in sharp contrast to the heavily centralised system operating six years ago. Then, production targets were set at the commune level and production brigades within each commune were given responsibility for the actual farming. Production surplus to the needs of the commune would be procured by the state at pre-ordained prices, with private plots strictly limited and offering no more than a marginal supplement to the basic diet.

The system now relies less on exhortation and more on incentives.[6] In addition to the encouragement of private markets, central government procurement prices have been increased by as much as 20 per cent; input costs, for fertiliser for instance, have been reduced; and procurement levels have been restrained to allow the retention of more grain in the rural areas. With limited information on the performance of the agricultural sector it is impossible to give a final assessment of the success of the modernisation programme. Certainly output of grain and of other products has risen and the development of private trading may conceivably leave published statistics understating the amount of output as more grain is used outside the public procurement and distribution programmes. The figures as published indicate a continuing growth of grain output but not the sudden surge of output hoped for by the proponents of liberalisation. Some reports have indicated the problems which remain — the substitution of lucrative cash crops for basic food production, the widening of income differentials in favour of farmers with better land and greater access to resources and the imposition of price increases on the urban consumer.

Liberalisation in any case has its limitations and the process is far from complete. For instance, though the work points which were the central feature of the old system have been replaced by production targets for families on particular areas of land, 'it is strenuously denied that the new system amounts to redistribution of land with the peasants becoming owners of the fields they farm. Land in theory is still owned by the collective . . . agriculture will generally continue to be small scale until the enhanced earnings of the country as a whole can finance the merging of land tracts'.[7]

These difficulties did not prevent the Chinese authorities setting ambitious targets amounting to production of 400 million tons per annum for the five-year-plan period ending in 1985. On the evidence of the last three years that target is now almost within reach. It is over the medium term in the period after 1985 that Chinese agricultural policy will face its real test. A series of problems remains unresolved and somewhat concealed by the effects of the limited liberalisation permitted since 1978. Land quality is poor beyond certain long cultivated regions. The most reliable indices of land use show an increase of only 17 per cent between 1952 and the late 1970s.[8] Less than 15 per cent of China's land area is cultivated. Additions to the cultivable land area are unlikely to be substantial. Chinese farmers have long been skilled in land use, and almost all reasonable land is under cultivation. Land use is far more intensive than in the United States or Europe. While in the United Kingdom or in the USA land may be normally left fallow on a regular basis, in China not only is most arable land cropped every year but some farmers rotate two, or even three different crops in the same year. Wheat and two varieties of rice may for example be cultivated in sequence on the same land in a single year. Such intensive land use is possibly only because of the careful husbandry which a large peasant labour force permits. Food and grain crops are likely to face competition for such land as is available from export crops, and in some areas from industrialisation. There is some scope for improvement in yields but although the Chinese have undertaken major developments in fertiliser production in the last ten years, the constraints of the volume required and of transportation will remain.

The climate adds to the difficulties facing the agricultural sector.

In the South, heavy rainfall occurs in the summer months when China forms part of the monsoon belt of East Asia. Beyond the high mountain ranges, the Centre and the North East tend to be too dry for sustained production, while the North China plains enjoy variable occasionally wet summers and dry winters. Much of the West is also dry. Very hot summers and long harsh winters provide little assistance to the farmer and the periodic drought which afflicts many parts of the country has set back plans for expanding and modernising the agricultural sector.

The lack of secure water supplies has been gradually but only partially countered and at a considerable cost in terms of resources. Chinese agriculture and food supply remain vulnerable to weather and climatic conditions. The extension of production to the North and the consequent reliance on essentially insecure supplies of water has increased vulnerability. At specific times and in specific regions over the last thirty years China has faced the very real prospect (and almost certainly the actuality) of famine on a significant scale. Irrigation is already of fundamental importance and the extension of land reclamation in the recent past, including, according to the IWC, land shaping — 'the levelling or terracing of whole mountains' — indicates that the limits of evolutionary improvements in output may be almost exhausted. Only very large-scale investment or the use of fertiliser and new higher yielding varieties of seed may be sufficient to maintain the momentum achieved in raising output.

There are also political limits to the process of privatisation. The idea of private accumulation regardless of the potential benefit in terms of output is still anathema and the ideology of centralised organisation under communism still retains a dominant influence over agricultural policy. The elements which have produced such advances in output in Western Europe and the USA — large-scale farms and a high degree of mechanisation, reflecting the substitution of capital for labour — appear to have no place in the Chinese strategy. The liberalisation seen since 1978 appears to have very clear limits, even under governments committed to national economic modernisation. It is not just these production constraints which suggest that China must turn to the outside world for agricultural supplies. A series of factors on the demand side narrow the options. Population growth remains an overriding factor in all calculations. The Chinese aim of reducing the growth to 1 per cent per annum may be achievable by the end of the century but at present it appears no more than a remote goal. The most recent World Bank estimates predict a slowing of growth in the period to the end of the century but not a sufficient slowing to prevent China having 250 million more mouths to feed by the year 2000.

Growth in the economy over the intervening period will add further pressure on the demand side. Chinese diets and nutrition levels are such that any increase in effective purchasing power is likely to be devoted to food consumption in the first instance. Even a small per capita increase, given China's population, would add very significantly to total demand. In Anthony Tang's words, 'since direct grain consumption is already adequate, especially in cities and farm areas with relatively high incomes, increased food consumption will consist primarily of meat and fruits which use more land, and in the case of meat, much more grain input for equivalent caloric production'.[9] Increases in the numbers of pigs and poultry to meet some of this increasing demand are already apparent, and the Chinese are devoting substantial resources to the development of a dairy industry.[10] The scale of the potential Chinese market is easily illustrated. Meat consumption is currently around 10 kg per capita according to the most recent FAO estimate against 57 kg per capita in the Soviet Union and 87 kg per capita in Australia. Population numbers according to the World Bank will be almost 1,250 million by 2000 even on their optimistic assumption that population growth will decline from its current level to an average of 1.2 per cent per annum between 1980 and 2000. China's urban population, predominantly in the North of the country, is currently some 130 million strong, and has been growing by 3 per cent per year in the 1970s. Some recent reports have indicated that the urban growth rate may now be being increased as a result of the new agricultural system which by enhancing the value of productivity is encouraging a shedding of agricultural labour.

The most thorough long-term forecast of Chinese needs, and of the ability of the country to meet them, has come from the International Food Policy Research Institute. Looking ahead, beyond the Chinese government's official target of 400 million tons of grain production by 1985, Anthony Tang bases his central forecasts on the calculation of gradual liberalisation of the economy, with an annual 2.5 per cent increase in household income and an income elasticity of demand for food of around 0.6 — a figure which itself is based on the assumption that a somewhat freer pattern of spending is permitted. Demand for foodgrains is projected to rise slowly at 2.1

per cent per annum — mainly under the pressure of population growth — with a much larger rate of increase for feed grains reflecting the use of increased consumer spending on meat products. Tang's calculation — of a 3 per cent per annum rise in the demand for grain indicates a required supply of some 538 million tons per annum by the year 2000.

As this study makes clear, this figure would be sharply increased (to as much as 800 million tons) if population control were unsuccessful or if a greater degree of liberalisation in matters of consumption were permitted. Equally if tight rationing were reintroduced demand could conceivably be limited to less than 400 million tonnes per year.

To achieve the supply indicated by the central estimate would require in Tang's view a growth of 6 per cent per annum of capital investment with a strong emphasis on farm machinery and a continuation of the policy indicated in the current ten-year plan of developing grassland for crop production on a large scale and opening up wasteland areas in the North East and the North West. Any extension of the land base could only increase the need for fertiliser. The current plan sets a goal of increasing domestic production by the establishment of at least one fertiliser plant — in each province by 1985, and the projection implies a required growth of 7 per cent per year in fertiliser use thereafter with the emphasis on chemical-based fertilisers. In volume terms that would mean output of 40 million tons per year by the end of the century against the 12 million tons produced in 1981.

On the record of the last ten years when chemical fertiliser use rose from 4.8 million tons in 1971 to over 12 million tons in 1981, such a growth rate is possible, even if fertiliser output of over 40 million tons per year at the end of the century may now seem wildly optimistic. Table 8.2 shows the extension of key agricultural imports in recent years. If such growth can be maintained the grain output targets for the end of the century and the intervening period would appear to be within reach. However, in Anthony Tang's words many questions remain:

What is the state of Chinese research in plant and animal breeding? How effective are the personnel, organization, and structure for research and development? What are the water prospects in Northern China where moisture is a chronic limiting factor? How do we evaluate the massive scheme to channel the

Table 8.2: Key Agricultural Imports

	1978	1979	1980	1981
000 units				
Large/medium sized tractors	557	667	745	792
Hand tractors	1,373	1,671	1,874	2,037
Drainage and irrigation machines	65,575	71,221	74,654	74,983
Million KwH				
Rural electricity consumption	25,300	28,300	32,100	37,000
000 tons				
Chemical fertiliser production	8,693	10,654	12,320	12,390

Source: USDA, *China. Review of Agriculture in 1981* (figures based on Chinese sources).

waters of the Yangste northward? Can the projected 7 per cent annual increase in current inputs be realized? Are there enough fertilizer plants in place and in process to meet the implicit chemical fertilizer requirement? How about energy and transport?

Faster population growth, energy shortage or a further political upheaval would also place the plans and targets in jeopardy. To maintain production and any sort of livestock sector China would be forced to import either grain or fertiliser or both on a significant scale if it were economically able to do so.

On both the supply and the demand side of the equation several key factors indicate that official optimism about the restoration and retention of self-sufficiency is overstated. As well as the heightened insecurity caused by reliance on imperfect growing areas, population growth, a more rapid degree of urbanisation, or the inability to sustain the necessary flow of resources into the agricultural sector might all force China to resort to the international market for its supplies on a regular basis.

Until now such trade as there has been has been defined as temporary and exceptional. Imports of grain began in a period of crisis in the early 1960s, and though they have grown since they have never been accepted as permanent. The sharp expansion of imports since the late 1970s has been presented as a deliberate policy exercise. Grain imported, first from Canada and Australia, and,

Table 8.3 Chinese Grain Imports from Major Suppliers

	1978/9	79/80	80/1	81/2	82/3	83/4
Argentina	0.9	0.5	0.2	0.3	2.2	1.1
Australia	1.4	3.7	1.4	1.5	1.0	1.8
Canada	3.2	2.6	2.9	3.1	4.2	3.8
EEC	—	0.1	0.6	0.1	1.4	0.1
USA	5.5	4.0	9.7	9.3	6.5	3.1
Total	11.2	10.9	14.8	14.7	15.6	10.1

Source: International Wheat Council, *Market Report*, various issues.

after the restoration of trade relations, from the United States has been used to supply the cities of the east coast to which internal supply lines are most limited and external supply lines most convenient. Imports have been used to maintain consumption through particular periods of supply shortage and more recently, as part of the evolving strategy of increasing domestic consumption through incentives, they have been used to allow farmers to retain a greater proportion of their own crops at commune level by reducing the central government call on their supplies. In addition China has been compelled to import large quantities of fertiliser to sustain the development of its farm sector and has now overtaken India as the world's leading fertiliser importer. Total use of all fertiliser had risen from approximately 90,000 tons in 1952 to over 15 million tons by the early 1980s. Fertiliser imports grew by 500 per cent between 1960 and the mid-1970s and one estimate covering the period from 1956 and 1976 concluded that they accounted for the equivalent of at least a further 12 million tons of grain imports each year.[11] The very rapid growth of the last five years suggests that that figure could now be doubled.

Even now, with medium-term supply agreements in operation, and covering the period to 1986, the trade position is presented as being no more than a passing phase and Chinese officials have even spoken hopefully of not only increased production sufficient to meet domestic needs but also of establishing an export capability in grain by 1990.[12] China, of course, remains a major exporter of agricultural products as well as an importer (Table 8.4).

Imports of cotton and of soyabeans, a crop long neglected by Chinese producers, have grown while the value of the traditional rice export crop has been limited by the very competitive market as supplies, not least from the US, increase and demand remains stagnant as diets improve and shift away from the traditional dependence on rice. Though China remains relatively minor in world grain market terms, her imports are of greater importance than the simple figures might suggest. Imported grain as a percentage of total consumption is still less than 5 per cent, but since most grain produced in China does not cross provincial boundaries, imports as a percentage of internally traded grain are substantial. Imports provide secure supplies to the cities and to the army — supplies which could only be matched by sharply increasing the call on communal production.

Since 1980 China has negotiated a series of short-term supply arrangements with the major exporting countries (Table 8.5). The

Table 8.4 Foreign Trade and Agriculture ($ million)

	1977	*1978*	*1979*	*1980*	*1981*
Total exports	8,101	10,118	13,751	19,493	22,400
Agricultural exports	2,648	3,118	3,629	4,327	4,900
Total imports	6,615	10,351	14,383	18,316	18,600
Agricultural imports	1,918	2,475	3,364	5,359	5,300
Trade balance	1,486	−233	−632	177	3,800
Agricultural trade balance	730	643	265	−1,032	−400

Source: USDA, *China. Review of Agriculture in 1981.*

Table 8.5 China: Import Commitments for Grain under Existing Agreements

Supplying country	Date announced	Duration Years	From	Quantities and specifications
Argentina	September 1980	4	1.1.81	0.7–0.9 million tons of wheat; and 0.3–0.6 million tons of maize (corn) and soyabeans annually
Australia	November 1981	3	1.1.82	1.5–2.5 million tons of wheat a year
Canada	May 1982	3	1.8.82	3.5–4.2 million tons of wheat annually
United States	October 1980	4	1.1.81	Minimum of 6 million tons, maximum 9 million tons of wheat and maize (corn) annually

Source: International Wheat Council, *Wheat Market Reports*, various issues.

most substantial of these deals are with Canada, to supply some 4 million tons of wheat each year, and with the United States, to supply a minimum of 6 and a maximum of 9 million tons of wheat and maize each year for four years from the beginning of 1981. Only recently have the arrangements begun to stretch beyond 1985.

Given the degree of control over systems of distribution exercised by the Chinese Government, it is of course conceivable that the central authorities will continue to restrict consumption, either for ideological reasons associated with an unwillingness to rely on 'free market' economic techniques, or to tolerate widening income differentials, and continued reliance on world markets, or for simple economic reasons associated with the balance of payments which might be unable to sustain large-scale imports on a regular basis.

This may in the end prove necessary, though the present commitment to incentives, which is at the heart of the government's policies for the industrial as well as the agricultural sector, implies rising disposable incomes, the most obvious use of which is increased consumption of food, and particularly meat.

Over time the pursuit of such policies might force upon Chinese governments the view that self-sufficiency is an over-rated objective. The cost both of resources and effort, and from a political perspective in terms of the degree of capital accumulation and incentive necessary to restructure Chinese production methods, may be found too great. Imports on a regular and accepted basis might offer a greater degree of stability and the opportunity for a greater independence of policy in respect of the development of the domestic economy.

This mixture of economic and political logic could make China within a decade the world's largest grain importer. Instead of declining, as presently anticipated by the government, import volumes of both wheat and coarse grain could grow, quite conceivably tripling from the levels of the early 1980s within ten years.

For the farmers of the world, beset by surpluses, budget constraints, a heavy overhead of stocks and low prices it is a tantalising prospect.

Notes

1. For example, in Bruce Stone, *A Review of Chinese Agricultural Statistics*, International Food Policy Research Institute, 1980, Washington DC and in B. Hay, 'Statistics on Food and Agriculture in China', *Food Policy*, November 1979.

2. C.P. Timmer, 'China and the World Food System' in R. Goldberg (ed.), *Research in Domestic and International Agribusiness Management*, Harvard, 1981.

3. The figure for 1983 is taken from the 1985 *World Development Report*, World Bank, Washington DC.

4. V. Smil, 'China's Food Availability', *Food Policy*, May 1981.

5. International Wheat Council, *Market Report*, March, 1985 reporting the statistics published by the Chinese State statistical bureau.

6. For a detailed description see T. Wiens, 'Chinese Economic Reforms. Price Adjustment, the Responsibility System and Agricultural Productivity', *American Economic Review*, May 1983.

7. *The Times*, London, 22 April 1983.

8. Anthony Tang and Bruce Stone, *Food Production in the People's Republic of China*, International Food Policy Research Institute, May 1980, Washington DC.

9. Ibid.

10. *Financial Times*, 27 December 1983.

11. Doak Barnett, *China and the World Food System*, Overseas Development Council, 1978, Washington DC.

12. For instance, Vice Premier Tian Jiyun quoted in *Financial Times* World Commodity Report, 11.7.84. In 1985 China exported a small volume of maize, mainly to Japan, but remained on balance a significant net importer.

9 PROSPECTS FOR THE WORLD GRAIN TRADE: THE SOUTH-EAST ASIAN MARKET

With all the indications suggesting that the current imbalance between supply and demand for grain will continue for the foreseeable future, and with a steady surplus both keeping prices down and forcing on governments measures such as the Payment in Kind programme in order to reduce output and stocks it is not surprising that the attention of farmers and traders is turning to the regions which seem to offer the best prospects for increases in demand in the medium- and long-term future.

Of all the Third World areas it is South East Asia which offers the brightest prospect. In the Latin American region indigenous supplies and potential are adequate to keep the major countries self-sufficient with a surplus available for export. Africa, though characterised by enormous potential demand, lacks the resources to make that demand effective either by agricultural development or by imports. Even Nigeria, once seen as a possible consumer of substantial quantities of traded grain is finding that falling oil revenues set a limit to import capabilities. With only one or two exceptions, any increase in consumption in the continent will be on the basis of improvements in home production or concessionary supplies.

In India, once a major grain importer, the remarkable advances in production techniques over the last decade have established something close to self-sufficiency as a normal outcome, despite steadily rising population and demand. Table 9.1 sets out the progress made.

India will still provide something of an outlet for the world grain trade but only on an irregular and erratic basis, when imports are needed to balance internal shortfalls.

By contrast in South East Asia a combination of circumstances indicates a potential market equal in extent to that provided by the centrally planned economies in the last decade. A handful of countries — Japan, South Korea, the Philippines, Indonesia, Malaysia, Thailand and Singapore — could provide the opportunity for trade running into tens of millions of tons of grain each year.

The first factor in the calculation is the rate of population growth.

145

Table 9.1 Food Grains in India (million metric tons)

Production	75/80 average	80/1	81/2	82/3	83/4	84/5 (estimate)
Total	119.6	129.6	133.3	128.4	151.5	150.5
of which wheat	31.0	36.3	37.5	42.5	45.1	46.0
rice	47.9	53.6	53.2	46.5	59.7	60.0
coarse grain	29.3	29.1	31.1	27.6	34.0	32.0
pulses	11.6	10.6	11.5	11.8	12.7	12.5
Net trade						
rice	+0.1	−0.9	−0.6	+0.2	+0.4	−0.3
wheat	+2.0	+0.4	+2.6	+4.2	+2.5	−0.5

Source: International Wheat Council, *Market Report*, July 1985. Imports + exports −.

Table 9.2 South East Asia: Population (millions)

	1984	Average Growth rate (% p.a.) 1980–2000	2000
Japan	118	0.4	128
South Korea	39	1.4	51
Indonesia	162	1.9	212
Malaysia	15	2.0	21
Thailand	50	1.9	68
Singapore	2	1.0	3
Philippines	53	2.1	73

Source: *World Development Report*, World Bank, 1984.

Table 9.3 GDP Per Capita

	GDP growth 1960/70	(% p.a.) 1970/82	GDP per capita (% p.a.) 1960/82	GDP per capita in US dollars 1982
Japan	10.4	4.6	6.1	10,080
S. Korea	8.6	6.6	6.6	1,910
Indonesia	3.9	7.7	4.2	580
Malaysia	6.5	7.7	4.3	1,860
Philippines	5.1	6.0	2.8	820
Thailand	8.4	7.1	4.5	790
Singapore	8.8	8.5	7.4	5,910
India	3.4	3.6	1.3	260
Egypt	4.3	8.4	3.6	690
UK	2.9	1.5	2.0	9,660
West Germany	4.4	2.4	3.1	12,460

Source: *World Development Report*, World Bank, 1984.

As a whole the region has one of the fastest population growth rates in the world. Table 9.2 shows the current and prospective populations on the most recent World Bank estimates. The figures take account of some decline in the growth rates from those seen in the recent past but still show an addition to the total population of almost 40 per cent over twenty years.

High population growth is not of course a feature unique to South East Asia. What is rare is the combination of such growth with a positive expansion of per capita income in each of the countries concerned over the last twenty years (Table 9.3).

The third factor arises from the increase in personal disposable income which is offered by these growth rates. Food consumption levels in South East Asia are still low on average — in some cases barely above the minimum standards of nutritional requirement. Average figures of course conceal wide variations from one area of a country to another and at different times during the year but they do show the general scope which exists for increasing the level of consumption.

Table 9.4 shows the levels of daily per capita calorie intake on the most recent estimate of the UN Food and Agriculture Organization.

The scope for increased demand associated with current and prospective per capita income, considered in conjunction with the demand arising from population growth itself, must strengthen the prospects of the area as the focus of growing food consumption.

From the traders' standpoint the most crucial factor is the way in which food demand will be met both in terms of content and source. In all the countries, including even Thailand which exports agricultural produce, the growth of the agricultural sector has been sacrificed to the pressures of industrialisation for the last two decades. In the 1970s in particular, agriculture declined as a source of national income, and as a provider of national food requirements.

Table 9.5 shows the pattern of change and Table 9.6 the growth of cereal imports as an indicator of the extent to which increased consumption has been import based, and funded by exports of industrial products and manufactured goods.

The major proportion of any increase in grain demand in South East Asia will come in the form of animal feed use. Rice is so well entrenched as part of the diet and so readily and inexpensively available that there appears to be little prospect of substantial

Table 9.4: Calorie Intake Per Capita, Per Day, 1981

	Nutritional requirement	Actual	Actual as a percentage of requirement
Japan	2,340	2,740	117
South Korea	2,350	2,931	126
Indonesia	2,160	2,342	110
Malaysia	2,230	2,662	121
Philippines	2,260	2,318	116
Thailand	2,220	2,303	105
Singapore	2,340	3,078	133
United States	2,631	3,647	138
West Germany	2,625	3,538	133

Source: *World Development Report*, World Bank, 1984. Nutritional requirements are as defined by the FAO.

Table 9.5: Agriculture in the Economy

	1970–82 Growth of output (% p.a.)		agriculture as a % of GDP	
	Agriculture	Industry	1960	1982
Japan	−0.2	5.6	13	4
South Korea	2.9	13.6	37	16
Indonesia	3.8	10.7	54	26
Malaysia	5.1	9.2	36	23
Philippines	−4.8	8.0	26	22
Thailand	4.4	9.3	40	22
Singapore	1.6	8.9	4	1

Source: *World Development Report,* World Bank, 1984.

Table 9.6: Volume of Cereal Imports (000 metric tons)

	1974	1982
Japan	19,557	24,336
South Korea	2,679	5,538
Indonesia	1,919	1,912
Malaysia	1,017	1,447
Philippines	817	1,287
Thailand	97	133
Singapore	682	1,819

Source: FAO; World Bank.

demand for breadmaking wheat. By contrast both the development of living standards and the insecurity of a key element of the present diet make some addition to the total demand for meat inevitable.

Meat consumption begins from a low base. As Table 9.7 shows, fish is still the predominant protein element in the diet of the region.

That combination of factors is the basis for the optimistic belief of some grain traders particularly in the United States but also in Australia and Europe that South East Asia will provide the salvation of an industry which could otherwise remain in a condition of semi-permanent slump relieved only by a major crop failure.[1]

By the end of the century according to this view exports to the Pacific nations will dominate the US grain trade. Japan alone will be importing 30 million tons and the other countries perhaps 15 million tons between them. On top of that will be added the Chinese market. Taken together such consumption levels would match at least current US production capabilities.

How realistic is the optimism and what is the timescale involved? To construct even a general forecast one must consider separately each of the factors involved.

Population numbers alone cannot provide an adequate forecasting tool by which to assess future levels of demand. By 1990 the population of the seven countries will be around 480 million, and by 2000 over 550 million, even assuming some slowing of the current rate of growth. Not all, however, will be adding to the demand for animal feed grain through the consumption of meat. In a number of countries, such as Indonesia which will see its population grow by a third in twenty years, tens of millions of people seem certain to remain remote from the sort of development implied by a westernised agricultural sector — the consumption of meat in processed forms. Demand for animal products will concentrate on the cities and the surrounding areas with many in the rural communities continuing to consume what is available locally through subsistence farming. Efforts to improve the efficiency and productivity of such farming will continue but even the most committed supporters of that process do not expect to see integrated national distribution networks incorporating every rural community established within the next two decades.

One of the delineations which the process of development is creating within the societies of the region will almost certainly be a sharp distinction in the patterns of food production and

Table 9.7: Per Capita Consumption of Livestock Products and Fish
(grams per day)

	Total	of which Fish	of which Meat
Japan	173	89	28
South Korea	66	32	13
Indonesia	20	10	4
Malaysia	111	67	22
Thailand	78	35	26
Philippines	78	34	19
Singapore	167	23	67

consumption between the populations of the urban and the rural areas.

Leaving aside Japan where a national distribution system does exist, demand for meat products will be concentrated in the cities of South East Asia, many of which are growing to enormous proportions (Table 9.8). It is of course in these cities that the greatest wealth from development will be accruing. By 2000 at least half of the population of South East Asia is likely to be living in urban areas. The growth in food demand will therefore be biased towards livestock products for consumption by the urban population.

The growth of GNP per capita for the urban population is likely to exceed the average for each country. Therefore even if current rates of growth are maintained, income per head in the urban population will rise sufficiently to permit increased expenditure on food.

The question of whether the rapid growth of the 1960s and 1970s

Table 9.8: Urbanisation

	Urban population as %age of total		Growth of Urban population (% per annum) 1960/82	Urban population 1982 (millions)
	1960	1982		
Japan	63	78	2.1	92
South Korea	28	61	4.6	24
Indonesia	15	22	3.6	34
Malaysia	25	30	3.3	4
Philippines	30	38	3.6	19
Thailand	13	17	3.4	8
Singapore	100	100	1.5	3

Source: *World Development Report*, World Bank, 1984.

will continue is thus less crucial than it might appear from calculations of individual demand, though it remains important because of the implications which grain imports carry for the balance of payments of every country concerned.

On the assumption that growth rates in the region maintain their levels of the last three to four years — well below the average of the last twenty years but still high in world terms — one might anticipate per capita income growth of 2–3 per cent per annum on average, perhaps 4 per cent per annum in the urban areas. The link to food demand then requires some estimate of the income elasticity of demand — the most difficult calculation of all given the lack of reliable historical data.

Taking such examples as are available, in particular the case of Japan which progressed through a similar stage of development, with comparable levels of per capita income some fifteen to twenty years ago, one can estimate, though without excessive confidence, that the income elasticity of demand might be of the order of at least 0.8 until per capita incomes reach the level of 3,000 dollars per annum in terms of the figures used in Table 9.3.

This suggests that overall food demand in the region is likely to increase by at least 3 per cent per annum between 1980 and 1990 and by a further 30 per cent before the end of the century, with the prospect of a greater increase if the distribution of income and income growth were to be more even. Though rice will remain the staple diet, its share of total calorie intake will fall as income is used to buy other forms of food.

Meat and fish will provide any improvement in the diet both in terms of quantity and quality. As things stand, fish is by far the dominant source of protein. Over recent years, however, successive reports have cast doubts on the ability of fish stocks to sustain the growth in per capita demand which income and population growth are creating. After rapid growth in the 1960s and early 1970s of well over 3 per cent per annum the growth of the world fish catch fell from the mid-1970s and is now barely 2 per cent per year.

Table 9.9 shows the development of fish catches by each of the South East Asian countries.

As well as the decline in the growth of the fish catches, legal limitations on fishing areas are bound to have a detrimental effect on availability for a number of the countries concerned. During the second half of the 1970s several of the countries, including Indonesia, Malaysia and the Philippines, imposed 200-mile limits to

Table 9.9: Fish Catch

	Percentage growth of total catch, 1973/81	Growth of catch, 1980/1	Catch, 1981 million metric tons
Japan	0.7 ˙	2.2	10.6
South Korea	6.2	13.1	2.4
Thailand	−0.2	−7.8	1.6
Philippines	3.0	6.0	1.65
Malaysia	7.5	8.0	0.8
Singapore	−1.7	0.4	0.01
Indonesia	4.9	1.2	1.9

Source: FAO, *The State of Food and Agriculture*, 1982.

protect their waters. The imposition of such zones by other countries has inevitably meant that for many of the nations dependent on fish a greater proportion of the total catch has to come from inshore waters in the future. The fact that the bulk of the catch still comes from outside territorial waters for each and every country including Japan, makes the general trend towards extensions of territorial limits a continuing threat. Indonesia takes only a quarter of its fish from inshore waters, Thailand 13 per cent and Japan and South Korea less than 2 per cent each.

There is also a clear need identified by each of the various international agencies involved for careful conservation of fish stocks, both in inshore waters and beyond. According to the FAO, the 1970s saw a continued increase in the number of fishing grounds being exploited beyond the maximum sustainable yield. The immediate pressures of demand in South East Asia and the Soviet Union in particular have led to public responses from both Japan and the USSR which suggest that the danger of continued overfishing is not yet fully appreciated.

To maintain the proportion of fish in the South East Asian diet at its current level would require an acceleration of the total catch — a trend in sharp contrast to the record of the recent past. Simple lack of supplies, or a rise in prices is likely instead to force a change in the diet. In the more developed countries of the region in particular the cost of maintaining expensive fishing fleets for limited returns may be judged excessive when set alongside the costs of developing new food supplies to meet common needs.

The process may be slowed by reluctance to accept the direction of change, but it seems certain that in ten years' time if not sooner fish will no longer hold the commanding position in the diet of the region.

Pork and poultry rather than beef are likely to supply the balance of demand. Such meat demand as exists is already biased in that direction, and beef has only a minimal share of the market, and of the traditional diet. Most of the beef now consumed in the region is part of the non-commercial food market with animals reared for local consumption only in the rural areas of Indonesia or Thailand.

The most important factor however is the lack of availability of suitable grazing land for cattle. Beef production is likely therefore to remain limited and to decline as a percentage of total demand except in the implausible circumstances of an increase in imports of meat products. Feed for poultry and pork will be required and provides the opportunity for the grain trade. Although the development of intensive production is not likely to proceed as rapidly as it has in Europe or the United States, the addition to grain demand which relatively inefficient production methods would offer (with a higher ratio of feed input to each unit of output), the involvement of Japanese, European and American companies in the sector might encourage the use of the most efficient methods in a relatively short time.

It is legitimate to be wary of over-precise numerical forecasts, given the scale of the various uncertainties involved. At present, imports into the region are limited and heavily concentrated on Japan, which takes 20 million tons of coarse grains and 6 million tons of wheat. In all, the region imports about a tenth of total world wheat trade of 97 million tons, and something over a quarter of world coarse grain trade of 88 million tons. But an orderly progression, with imported grain supplying the needs of a substantial indigenous livestock sector by the end of the century, is far from certain or predetermined. First, real balance of payments problems may deny any or all the countries involved the resources necessary to establish a large-scale reliance on commodity imports. Competition for Western markets in labour-intensive manufactures and in a succession of electronic products is fierce and involves not just the South East Asian countries concerned but also countries in Latin America, parts of Africa and in other parts of Asia. Only a rapidly growing world economy with Europe, the United States and Japan itself open and receptive to trade and economic restructuring will allow all the countries concerned to prosper. Even then, and certainly in conditions short of that rapid growth, there is no guarantee that all the countries of the region will continue in the heady manner of the last decade. One or two may acquire an advantage which attracts capital and concentrates technical progress in a way not envisaged after the general and widespread successes of the last two decades.

Beyond the general problem, individual economies face particular difficulties. The political stability which some economists seem to take for granted cannot be guaranteed. In the Philippines the events following the assassination of Benito Aquino in August 1983 showed the fragility of a populous society divided by custom and religion.

In Thailand the almost annual change of government creates a sense of normality in disorder but the nature of the surrounding countries and the dependence even now on a few key crops and products means that the sense of order and progress established since the mid-1970s could be disrupted badly in particular circumstances. For Indonesia the fall in the price of oil has reduced export earnings and investment capabilities, and may have removed one of the elements concealing the inequities and divisions in a society where the urban-rural distinctions are at their sharpest. Dramatic population growth creates basic requirements for employment, land and food which even the essentially pragmatic Suharto regime will not be able to accommodate if oil export revenues really have peaked. The future of Hong Kong, and the prospects for political stability in continued exported growth in Japan and South Korea are beyond the scope of this study, but the air of uncertainty surrounding both in recent years only adds to the risk that the easy answer to the problems of surplus in the grain market offered by continuing dynamic growth in seven or eight countries in one region may be over-optimistic.

The third risk which might arise even if growth persists is that the individual countries of the region will be reluctant to permit the further decline in the level of their self-sufficiency in key supplies. The Japanese literature on the need to avoid import dependence, whether in oil or food is now substantial and the strength of the argument has been diminished only marginally by the fall in prices.

Given a surplus of rice on the world market[2] each of the countries may choose to restrict imports of grain and to encourage the use of rice through a mixture of tariffs and subsidies. Imported grain would then remain the exception rather than the norm, and a feature of the diet of the minority rather than a feature of a new staple diet for all.

Economic circumstances in the region and in the rest of the world will be the main conditioning factors. A recovery without a further leap in oil prices would facilitate trade and would encourage a transition to a new pattern of food consumption. Instability or a slump in trade would put imported food beyond the means of many of the countries of South East Asia.

Notes

1. USDA Economic Research Service, *Southeast Asia Outlook and Situation Report*, June 1985.
2. A. Siamwalla, *The World Rice Market*, International Food Policy Research Institute, Washington DC, 1983.

10 CONCLUSION

The focus of this book has been international markets for grain. The problems set out — of overheavy stocks, of low prices, of excessive costs of intervention, and of farm incomes which remain low — are the subject of constant proposals for change and reform from political parties, academics, farm organisations and governments.

At the time of writing, the summer of 1985, there are significant reform proposals on the table in both the main exporting areas — the USA and the EEC. The US Government in part at least is seeking to reduce dramatically its financial commitment to agriculture as one part of its strategy of bringing down the US budget deficit. The European Community, seeing ahead the problems of enlargement and of growing output in both the existing members and in those now joining, is seeking means to limit the costs to the European budget of intervention buying and export subsidies. Without some limitation the costs of the CAP will rise inexorably and consume all the additional resources accruing to the EEC from the increase in the contributions of members states.

In the Soviet Union too, a new measure of reform is likely in the twelfth five-year plan. Along with energy, agriculture must be the civilian priority of the new regime and we can expect both the continuation of existing high levels of investment and some attempt to reform the links with the industrial and the distributional elements of the system, even if a fundamental reform of the overall Soviet agriculture management regime still seems unlikely.

In all three cases a degree of scepticism about the reform proposals is justified. In the Soviet Union admirable objectives backed by high spending have been set out in planning documents on numerous previous occasions. Agriculture has been given a priority quite unknown thirty or forty years ago. The satisfaction of consumer demands has been recognised as a necessary and legitimate goal of communism. Yet grain output is lower than it was ten years ago and imports are at an all-time high.

For the USA, reform presents difficulties which are not ideological but political. Proposals to cut farm spending by reducing support prices have been fiercely resisted and are unlikely to be sustained through the congressional election year of 1986 let alone the presidential election year of 1988. The farmers of the Midwest whose life is dominated by the threat of foreclosure by banks whose credit has been overextended are now the new poor of the United States. One can only doubt the political will of any administration which is apparently prepared to risk a significant exodus from farming. The European Commission likewise faces enormous difficulty if it seeks to alter fundamentally the system of price support which has underpinned the CAP. The example set in the early months of 1985 by the German Farm Minister in opposing even a minor cut (of 1.8 per cent) in the support prices of grain because of its effect on the living standards (and voting intentions) of those engaged in small-scale farming operations in Germany is just one well-publicised example of the general trend in the Community decision-making process which sustains the status quo as a starting point and then reaches consensus between countries by means of concession to the highest demand.

Small cuts in support prices and even schemes which penalise production over fixed limits have stemmed the overall rise in Community agricultural spending. New proposals to create new internal uses for surplus grain — for instance in the production of ethanol — would do no more than shift the burden of that expenditure from one budget heading to another.

The most serious weakness of all the proposals currently under discussion, however, is their disregard for the effect on the international market not just of the existing problems but also of the proposed solutions.

The US scheme to dispose of surplus stocks and to win back markets lost to 'unfair competition' would if pushed weaken prices and reduce the income per ton of all traders including US traders themselves. Taken to its limit it would probably provide a competition in subsidies helpful to a few importers but damaging in terms of resources wasted and wider trade relations. Given its underlying budget problems there is no guarantee that the USA could even win such a contest in macho economics.

The EEC's proposals — to divert grain back into the domestic market or to seek long-term trading deals with key importers — take an equally cavalier view of the international market and merely institutionalise an internal problem by exporting the difficulty or by cutting off even more of the already falling import trade.

The winners and losers from these policies would be found in the countries of the developing world, as well as within the USA and the European Community countries themselves. Significant grain importing countries such as Egypt would undoubtedly benefit from the buyers' market and the competition between governments to supply them. As things stand there are significantly more importers than exporters but this simple first-order effect is probably outweighed by other and more adverse consequences.

The most successful developing countries in terms of grain production and agricultural development generally have been those which have minimised imports (such as India) or those which have used limited imports as no more than one instrument of resource management (such as China). Both countries have succeeded in raising their grain production and improving yields at rates well above the world average. Below the average come the countries which have failed to develop their own agricultural sectors and which have relied on imported grain at relatively cheap prices as their basic source of supply. In times of balance of payments difficulty — caused by trends in other commodity prices, from oil on the import side to tin and rubber as exports — the ability to buy imported grain is constrained. Too many countries have found in such circumstances that their indigenous agricultural sector is too limited to provide balancing supplies.

This book is not about food aid or about the various proposals, some excellent and sadly neglected, for insurance schemes, international stocks and other devices to ensure that in times of crisis or difficulty basic supplies are maintained. Although such schemes are important they are at best no more than a complement to the development of viable agricultural sectors within developing countries themselves. In some cases land availability or the sheer weight of population makes self-sufficiency unattainable or undesirably expensive, but in many countries, especially in Africa, the potential is far greater than the current achievement.

Not all the problems of agriculture in the developing countries can be traced back to the CAP or to the agricultural and trade policies of the main actors in the world market. Poor management, misused tax and incentive systems and the diversion of resources to cash crops such as tobacco all play their part.

Nevertheless, those whose policies dominate the world market and who therefore set the incentives and objectives for Third World producers — whether importers or exporters — have a responsibility to judge those policies and any proposed reforms in a context which is wider than that of purely domestic interest. Thus as a starting point reform would be better undertaken as a collective exercise than as a series of individual national or community level measures. Between the USA and the EEC a collective reform could involve trade-offs which might be beneficial internationally but there would clearly be a greater benefit in involving other producers and consumers in the exercise.

The principles of reform should be:

The establishment of a ceiling on subsidies by exporters, with the ceiling phased down over a period of years.

The distribution for a temporary period of quotas within the world market, including quotas for growth.

Agreement on the holding (and distribution of costs) of stocks coupled if possible with internationally managed reserves for use in times of emergency.

Renewal of the commitments made in the 1970s to assist agricultural development by transfer of appropriate technology to developing countries, along with the provision of training in the use and adaptation of that technology.

Having set out all the difficulties facing current reform proposals, this programme sounds Utopian indeed, especially as the transition phases are designed to end in something much closer to an open market.

There is, however, an important common interest among producers and consumers on all sides of the market. Under the present proposals for reform coming from the USA and the EEC, the imbalance between available supply and effective demand is to be corrected simply by reducing available supply. The US proposals would reduce price levels and clear farmers off the land — a humane set aside programme. EEC proposals would direct grain to internal and non-food uses and in so far as lower support prices discourage production it would cut or restrain output.

The alternative means of closing the gap between supply and demand is to increase effective demand so that a greater proportion of the supply which modern agriculture can provide can be absorbed.

It would be foolish to lay the blame for the present imbalance on the technical advances and high productivity achievements of farmers in Western Europe or the United States. Only if demand is regarded as static and no effort is made to translate latent or potential demand into effective purchases can the agricultural problems of the 1980s be defined in terms of oversupply.

Demand can be stimulated, and made effective and the scale of need is such that both indigenous development within the Third World countries and imports would be necessary if nutritional standards in Africa and Asia were raised to even the bottom end of the scale of what would be acceptable in Europe or the United States. That goal, however distant, should be established as the objective in all attempts to resolve the current problems.

SUMMARY TABLES

Table 1: Wheat (million metric tons)

	Production	Consumption	Trade	Trade as % of production
1946–51 av.	154	152	24	16
1951–56 av.	196	186	26	13
1956–61 av.	237	232	37	16
1961–66 av.	253	256	52	21
1966–71 av.	315	312	52	17
1971–76 av.	360	362	62	17
1976–81 av.	427	422	77	18
1981/82	454	447	101	22
1982/83	483	456	96	20
1983/84	496	485	99	20
1984/85	521	495	104	20
1985/86 (est)	510	507	88	17

Table 2: Wheat: Yields

Quintals (100kg/ha)	1970/75 av.	1976/80 av.	1981	1982	1983
EEC	35.5	39.4	42.8	46.1	45.0
Total Western Europe	30.1	34.8	36.7	40.2	39.5
Eastern Europe	28.6	33.7	34.1	37.3	35.2
USSR	14.6	16.4	13.5	16.3	15.7
Canada	17.2	18.9	20.0	21.3	19.6
USA	21.0	21.5	23.2	23.9	26.5
Argentina	14.8	16.1	14.0	20.5	17.9
Asia	12.5	15.7	17.6	18.9	20.8
India	12.8	14.6	16.3	16.9	18.4
China	14.6	18.2	21.1	24.5	28.6
Australia	12.3	12.9	13.8	7.7	17.3
Total world	16.2	18.4	18.9	20.2	21.6

Table 3: Basic Support Levels for Wheat (US $ per metric ton)

	1978/79	*79/80*	*80/81*	*81/82*	*82/83*	*83/84*
EEC	213	229	247	229	201	197
Spain	206	227	193	176	155	155
Canada	98	133	164	145	140	138
USA	125	125	134	140	149	158
Argentina	124	122	196	172	78	98
India	135	139	141	159	152	151
Australia	105	126	154	161	134	137

Note: The prices are those used as a basis for government guaranteed prices and are not necessarily comparable between nations. National currency support levels are converted as IMF par values and where not available at IMF exchange rates for the first month of the country's crop year.

Table 4: Production: Coarse Grains (million metric tons)

	1970/71	*80/81*	*82/83*	*83/84*	*84/85*
EEC[a]	37.3	69.4	71.4	64.2	75.1
Total Western Europe	74.5	105.1	105.4	98.1	116.7
Eastern Europe	36.3	51.4	58.5	55.6	59.9
USSR	76.3	80.6	85.0	105.0	85.0
Canada	19.6	21.8	26.7	21.0	21.9
USA	144.5	198.4	254.2	137.1	237.1
Argentina	15.6	21.5	18.1	18.0	20.2
Brazil	15.4	23.0	20.0	21.5	22.0
China	75.0	85.0	85.0	92.0	95.0
India	28.6	28.4	28.2	34.0	33.0
Africa	46.6	56.0	45.0	41.2	43.9
Australia	4.5	5.2	3.7	9.5	9.3
World Total	591.1	732.6	785.5	691.3	801.1

Note: a. Refers to EEC's 6 members in 1970/71. 10 members thereafter.

Table 5: Production: Wheat (million metric tons)

	1970/71	74/75	79/80	82/83	83/84	84/85
EEC (10)	36.6	47.5	48.8	59.9	59.2	76.3
France	12.9	19.1	19.5	25.4	24.8	33.2
UK	4.2	6.1	9.0	10.3	10.8	15.0
Eastern Europe	19.2	27.9	23.2	29.4	29.9	34.8
USSR	99.7	83.9	90.2	85.0	80.0	75.0
Canada	9.0	13.3	77.6	26.8	26.6	21.2
USA	36.8	48.5	58.1	76.5	65.9	70.6
Argentina	4.9	6.0	8.1	15.0	12.3	13.2
China	31.0	40.9	62.7	68.4	81.4	87.8
India	20.1	21.8	35.5	37.5	42.8	45.5
Australia	7.9	11.4	16.2	8.9	21.9	18.3
World Total	318.9	363.8	428.8	483.5	495.9	521.4

Soviet figures for the years after 1980 are estimates from the IWC.

Note (a) Refers to the EEC's six members in 1970, nine members in 1974/79, ten members thereafter.

Table 6: Coarse Grains: Exports (million metric tons)

Main exporters	1979/80	80/81	83/84	84/85
Argentina	6.6	9.9	12.0	10.6
Australia	4.0	2.2	4.3	7.6
Canada	4.9	4.7	6.7	3.8
EEC[a]	3.4	4.5	3.0	8.0
Thailand	2.1	2.1	3.1	3.4
USA	71.6	72.6	55.5	58.4
Total	98.2	102.6	91.0	101.9

Note: a. EEC figures exclude intra-EEC trade.

Table 7: Coarse Grains: Imports (million metric tons)

Main Importers	*1976/77*	*79/80*	*80/81*	*83/84*	*84/85*
EEC[a]	26.7	12.2	12.8	5.5	3.9
Spain				5.1	2.8
Eastern Europe	8.2	10.4	9.6	3.8	3.6
USSR	6.7	18.7	18.0	11.6	27.7
Mexico				6.3	4.8
China	—	2.0	1.0	0.4	0.4
Japan	15.9	19.0	18.8	20.5	21.0
South Korea				4.0	3.5
Total Far East	23.6	32.8	31.9	31.1	31.2
Egypt				1.5	1.7
South Africa				3.3	1.2
Saudi Arabia				5.0	5.5
Total	79.6	99.0	101.1	91.0	101.9

Note (a) EEC figures exclude intra-EEC trade. 1976/77 and 1979/80 are for EEC 9. EEC 10 thereafter.

Table 8: Wheat: Exports (million metric tons)

	1970/71	*74/75*	*79/80*	*82/83*	*83/84*	*estimated* *84/85*
Argentina	1.7	2.2	4.7	7.5	9.6	7.9
Australia	9.5	8.0	15.4	8.5	11.6	15.1
Canada	11.6	11.2	15.0	21.1	21.2	19.2
EEC[a]	3.1	7.1	10.3	14.1	15.0	16.9
USA	19.8	28.3	36.6	39.3	38.3	37.9
World total	54.3	63.4	86.0	96.1	100.4	105.1

Note: a. EEC figures exclude intra-EEC trade. 1970/71 figures are for EEC 6, 1974/75 and 1979/80 for EEC 9, thereafter for EEC 10.

Table 9:   Wheat: Imports (million metric tons)

	1970/71	74/75	79/80	82/83	83/84	84/85
Main importers						
EEC[a]	4.4	5.2	4.5	3.4	3.5	2.5
UK	5.1	3.4	1.7	1.1	1.0	0.7
Eastern Europe	5.8	3.7	5.3	3.9	3.5	2.8
USSR	0.3	2.8	11.7	20.1	20.6	28.3
Middle East	4.6	6.1	7.5	8.0	10.8	12.2
Far East	17.8	27.3	25.3	32.3	28.0	25.0
of which						
China	3.7	5.3	8.7	13.0	9.8	7.7
India	2.2	6.2	0.2	4.3	2.5	0.1
Japan	4.7	5.3	5.6	5.6	5.9	6.1
Africa	7.0	9.0	13.8	15.0	18.5	19.0
of which						
Egypt	3.0	3.4	5.2	6.2	7.3	7.0
World total	54.3	63.4	86.0	96.9	100.4	105.1

Note: a. EEC figures exclude intra-EEC trade.   1970/71 figures are for EEC 6, 1974/75 and 1979/80 for EEC 9, thereafter for EEC 10. Figures for wheat trade include wheat flour.

BIBLIOGRAPHY

Articles

Barraclough, G., 'Wealth and Power: The Politics of Food and Oil', *New York Review of Books*, New York, 7 August 1975

Bigman, D. and Reutlinger, S., 'National and International Policies Toward Food Security and Price Stabilisation', *American Economic Review*, May 1979.

Brown, Lester R., 'Soils and Civilization: The Decline in Food Security', *Third World Quarterly*, January 1983

Destler, I.M., 'United States Food Policy 1972–76: Reconciling Domestic and International Objectives', *International Organisation*, 32, Summer 1978

Eicher, Carl K., 'Africa's Food Crisis', *Foreign Affairs*, Fall 1982, vol. 61, no. 1

Gilmore, Richard, 'Grain in the Bank', *Foreign Policy*, no. 38, Spring 1980

Hadja, J., 'The Soviet Grain Embargo', *Survival*, Nov./Dec. 1980

Johnson, D. Gale, 'Limitations of Grain Reserves in the Quest for Stable Prices', *World Economy*, June 1978

Josling, T.E., 'Agriculture's Place in General Economic Policy', *The World Economy*, October 1977

Koester, Ulrich, 'Controlled Nationalization of Agricultural Policy in the EC', *Intereconomics*, March/April 1981, Hamburg

——, 'The Chances for a Thorough Reform of The EC's Common Agricultural Policy', *Intereconomics*, January/February 1981, Hamburg

Martens, Laurent, 'Part time farming in developed countries', *European Review of Agricultural Economics*, 7 (1980)

Nove, Alec, 'Soviet Agriculture. New Data', *Soviet Studies*, 34 (1), January 1982

Paarlberg, R., 'Food, Oil and Coercive Resource Power', *International Security*, vol. 3, no. 2, Fall 1978

——, 'Lessons of the Grain Embargo', *Foreign Affairs*, Fall 1980

——, 'The Soviet Burden on the World Food System: Challenge and Response', *Food Policy*, November 1976

Rankin, J., 'The Grain Embargo', *Washington Quarterly*, Summer 1980

Rollo, J.M. and Warwick, G., 'The Second Enlargement of the EEC', *Journal of Agricultural Economics*, 1979

Rothschild, Emma, 'Food Politics', *Foreign Affairs*, vol. 54. no 3, January 1976

Sen, A., 'The Food Problem — Theory and Policy', *Third World Quarterly*, July 1982

Smil, V., 'China's Food Availability, Requirements, Composition and Prospects', *Food Policy*, May 1981

Soth, Lauren, 'The Grain Export Boom', *Foreign Affairs*, vol. 59, no. 4, Spring 1981

Swinbank, A., 'European Community Agriculture and the World Market', *American Journal of Agricultural Economics*, vol. 62, no. 3, August 1980

Tang, A., 'China as a Factor in the World Food Situation', *American Journal of Agricultural Economics*, May 1982

Tangerman, Stefan, 'Agricultural Trade Relations between the EC and Temperate Food Exporting Countries', *European Review of Agricultural Economics*, 5 (nos. 3–4, 1978)

——, 'EEC Agricultural Trade Policy and International Responsibilities', *World Agriculture*, 1979

Timmer, C.P., 'China and the World Grain Market', *Challenge*, September/October 1981

Wadekin, Karl-Eugen, 'Soviet Agriculture and the West', *Foreign Affairs*, Spring 1982, vol. 60, no. 4

Wagstaff H., 'EEC Food Surpluses: Controlling Production by Two Tier Prices', *National Westminster Bank Quarterly Review*, November 1982

Wallerstein, M., 'Dynamics of Food Policy Foundation in the USA', *World Economy*, August 1982

Warley, T.K., 'What Chance has Agriculture in the Tokyo Round?', *World Economy*, 1977 (1)

Wiens, T., 'Chinese Agriculture: Continued Self Reliance', *American Journal of Agricultural Economics*, December 1978

——, 'Price Adjustment, the Responsibility System and Agricultural Productivity in China', *American Economic Review*, May 1983

Yergin, Daniel, 'Politics and Soviet American Trade: The Three Questions', *Foreign Affairs*, vol. 55/3, April 1977

Zagoria, Donald S., 'China's Quiet Revolution', *Foreign Affairs*, vol. 62, no. 4, Spring 1984

Books and Papers

Ali, L., *The World Wheat Market and International Agreements*, UNCTAD, Geneva, 1982

Averyt, William F., *Agropolitics in The European Community Interest Groups and the CAP*, Praegar, New York, 1977

Balaam D.N. and Carey M.J., *Food Politics: The Regional Conflict*, Croom Helm, London, 1981

Bana, Tibor, *Agriculture towards the Year 2000*, Sussex European Research Centre, University of Sussex, 1979

Barker, R. and Sinha, R. (eds), *Cornell Workshop on Agricultural and Rural Development in the People's Republic of China*, Cornell University, New York, 1979

Barnett A. Doak, *China and the World Food System*, Overseas Development Council, Washington, DC, April 1979

——, *China's Economy in Global Perspective*, Brookings Institution, Washington, DC, 1980

Body, Richard, *Agriculture — The Triumph and the Shame*, Temple Smith, London, 1982

Brown, Lester R., *The Politics and Responsibility of the North American Breadbasket*, Worldwatch Institute Paper No. 2, Washington, DC, 1975

——, *US and Soviet Agriculture: The Shifting Balance of Power*, Worldwatch Institute, Washington, DC, October 1982

Buckwell, Harvey and Thompson, *The Costs of the CAP*, Croom Helm, London, 1982

Burback, R. and Flynn, P., *Agribusiness in the Americas*, Monthly Review Press, New York, 1980

Business Week, *Food Power: The Ultimate Weapon in World Politics*, December 15, 1975, pp. 54–60

Castle, Emery N. and Hemi, Kenzo, *US–Japanese Agriculture Trade Relations*, Resources for the Future, Washington, DC, 1982

Clay, Edward and Singer, Hans, *Food as Aid: Food for Thought*, I.D.S. Bulletin, vol. 14, no. 2, Sussex, 1983

Cohen, Stephen D., *The Making of United States International Economic Policy* (2nd edn), Praegar, New York, 1981

Commission of the European Community, *The Agricultural Situation in the Community*, various issues, European Commission, Brussels, various years

——, *Reflections on the Common Agricultural Policy*, European Commission, Brussels, 1980

Crosson, Pierre R., *The Cropland Crisis — Myth or Reality?*, Resources for the Future, Washington, DC, 1982

Crosson, Pierre R. and Frederick, Kenneth D., *The World Food Situation: Resource and Environmental Issues in the Developing Countries and the United States*, Resources for the Future, Washington, DC, 1977

Davey, T., Josling, T.E. and McFarquahar, R., *Agriculture and the State: British Policy in a World Context*, Macmillan, London, 1976

Desai, Padma, *Estimates of Soviet Grain Imports in 1980–85*, IFPRI Research Report 22, Washington, DC, 1981

Destler, I.M., *Making Foreign Economic Policy*, Brookings Institution, Washington, DC, 1980

Food and Agriculture Organization of the UN, *Agriculture. Towards 2000*, FAO, Rome, 1979

——, *Production Yearbook*, various issues, FAO, Rome, various years

——, *The State of Food and Agriculture*, various issues, FAO, Rome, various years

——, *Trade Yearbook*, various issues, FAO, Rome, various years

Food and Fertilizer Technology Center, *Food Situation and Potential in the Asian and Pacific Region*, Food and Fertilizer Technology Center, Taipei, Taiwan, 1980

Fraenkel, R.M., Hadwiger, D.F. and Browne, W.P., *The Role of US Agriculture in Foreign Policy*, Praeger, New York, 1979

Francisco, R., Laird, B.A. and Laird, R.D., *Agricultural Policies in Eastern Europe and the USSR*, Westview, Boulder, Colorado, 1980

GATT, *International Trade*, annual, various issues, GATT, Geneva, various years

——, *The Tokyo Round of Multilateral Trade Negotiations*, GATT, Geneva, 1979

Gilmore, Richard, *A Poor Harvest. The Clash of Policies and Interests in the Grain Trade*, Longman, London, 1982

Goldberg, R.A. (ed.), *Research in Domestic and International Agribusiness Management*, Jai Press Inc., Greenwich, Connecticut, 1980, 1981

Goreux, Louis M., *Compensatory Financing Facility*, International Monetary Fund, Pamphlet Series 34, Washington, DC, 1980

Grennes, T., Johnson P.R. and Thursby, M., *The Economics of World Grain Trade*, Praegar, New York, 1978

Guither, Harold D., *The Food Lobbyists*, Lexington Books, Lexington, Mass., 1980

Harris, Simon, *EEC Trade Negotiations with the USA in Agricultural Products*, Centre for European Agricultural Studies, University of London, Ashford, Kent, 1977

Hedland, Stefan, *Crisis in Soviet Agriculture*, Croom Helm, London, 1984

Heidhues, T., *World Food. Interdependence of Farm and Trade Policies*, Trade Policy Research Centre, London, 1977

Hillman, J.S., *Non Tariff Agricultural Trade Barriers*, University of Nebraska Press, Lincoln, 1978

Hillman, J.S. and Schmitz, A. (eds), *International Trade and Agriculture Theory and Policy*, Westview, Boulder, Colorado, 1979

Hopkins, R.F. and Puchala, D.J., *Global Food Interdependence: Challenge to American Foreign Policy*, Columbia UP, New York, 1980

——, *The Global Political Economy of Food*, University of Wisconsin Press, Madison, 1978

House of Lords Select Committee on the European Communities, *Agricultural*

Trade Policy, HMSO, 1981
——, *Development Aid Policy*, HMSO, London, 1981
——, *Imports of Cereal Substitutes*, HMSO, London, 1981
——, *The Common Agricultural Policy*, HMSO, London, 1980
——, *The Common Agricultural Policy — Directions of Future Development and Proposals for Prices and Related Measures*, HMSO, London, 1981
——, *Trade Patterns. The UK's Changing Trade Patterns Subsequent to Membership of the European Community*, HMSO, London, 1983
Huddleston, Barbara, *Closing the Cereals Gap with Trade and Food Aid*, IFPRI Research Report 43, Washington, DC, 1984
Huddleston, Barbara and McLin, J. (eds), *Political Investments in Food Production*, Indiana University Press, Bloomington, 1979
International Food Policy Research Institute, *Food Needs of Developing Countries: Projections of Production and Consumption to 1990*, IFPRI, Washington, DC, 1977
International Wheat Council, *Annual Report*, various issues, IWC, London, various years
——, *World Wheat Statistics*, various issues, IWC, London, various years
Jabara, Cathy L., *Trade Restrictions in International Grain and Oilseed Markets*, USDA Economics and Statistics Service, Report No. 162, Washington, DC, 1981
Jabara, Cathy L. and Brigida, Alan S., *Variable Levies. Barriers to Grain Imports in France, Netherlands, Federal Republic of Germany and United Kingdom*, ESCS/USDA, Foreign Agricultural Economic Report No. 156, March 1980
Jackson, Tony, *Against the Grain: The Dilemma of Proper Food Aid*, Oxfam, Oxford, 1982
Johnson, D. Gale, *The Soviet Impact on World Grain Trade*, British North America Committee, London, 1977
Johnson, D. Gale (ed.), *Food and Agricultural Policy for the 1980s*, American Enterprise Institute, Washington, DC, 1981
——, *The Politics of Food*, Chicago Council on Foreign Relations, Chicago, 1980
Johnson, D. Gale and Schuh, G.E. *The Role of Markets in the World Food Economy*. Westview. Boulder, Co. 1983
Johnson, D. Gale and Schutz, G. Edward (eds), *The Role of Markets in the World Food Economy*, Westview, Boulder, Colorado, 1983
Jones, David, *Food and Interdependence. The Effect of Food and Agricultural Policies of Developed Countries on the Food Problems of Developing Countries*, London, ODI, 1976
Josling, T.E., *Agriculture in the Tokyo Round Negotiations*, Trade Policy Research Centre, Thames Essay No. 10, London, 1977
——, *Developed Country Agricultural Policies and Developing Country Supplies: The Case of Wheat*, IFPRI Research Report 14, Washington, DC, 1980
——, *Problems and Prospects for US Agriculture in World Markets*, NPA, Washington, DC, 1981
Koester, Ulrich, *Policy Options for the Grain Economy of the European Community: Implications for Developing Countries*, IPRI Research Report 35, Washington, DC, 1982
Konandreus, P., Huddleston, B. and Virabongsa, R., *Food Security: An Insurance Approach*, IFPRI Research Report 4, Washington, DC, 1978
Marsh, J.S., *UK Agricultural Policy within the European Community*, Centre for Agricultural Strategy, Paper No. 1, Reading, UK, 1977
Ministry of Agriculture, Fisheries and Food, *Annual Review of Agriculture*, various issues, HMSO, London, various years
——, *Farming and the Nation*, CMND 7458, HMSO, London, 1979
Morgan, Dan, *Merchants of Grain*, Viking, New York, 1979

Morris, C.N., *CAP: Structures and Methods*, Institute for Fiscal Studies, London, March, 1980

Morrow, Daniel T., 'The International Wheat Agreement and LDC Food Security' in A. Valdes (ed.), *Food Security for Developing Countries*, Westview, Boulder, Colorado, 1981

——, *The Economics of the International Stockpiling of Wheat*, IFPRI Research Report 18, Washington, DC, 1980

OECD, *Food Policy*, OECD, Paris, 1981

——, *Prospects for Agricultural Production and Trade in Eastern Europe*, OECD, Paris, 1981

——, *Prospects for Soviet Agricultural Production and Trade*, OECD, Paris, 1983

——, *Prospects for Soviet Agricultural Production in 1980 and 1985*, OECD, Paris, 1979

——, *The Instability of Agricultural Commodity Markets*, OECD, Paris, 1980

Ogura, Takekazu, *Can Japanese Agriculture Survive?*, Agricultural Policy Research Center, Tokyo, 1980

Paarlberg, R., 'A Food Security Approach for the 1980s' in *US Policy and the Third World. Overseas Development Council*, Praegar, New York, 1982

——, *Farm and Food Policy: Issues of the 1980s*, University of Nebraska, 1980

——, *Food Trade and Foreign Policy*. Cornell. 1985

Parikh, K. and Rabar, F., *Food for All in a Sustainable World. The IIASA Food and Agriculture Program*, IIASA, Vienna, 1981

Pearce, J., *The Politics of the CAP*, Royal Institute of International Affairs, London, 1981

Renwick, R., *Economic Sanctions*, Harvard University Press, Cambridge, Mass., 1981

Ritson, C., *Self Sufficiency and Food Security*, Centre for Agricultural Strategy, Paper No. 8, Reading, UK, 1979

Ruhter-Altsehaffer, J.H., *Agriculture as a Problem in the Relations between Europe and the United States*, Sage Publications, Washington Papers vol. 2.2, Beverly Hills, 1974

Sanderson, Fred H., *Japan's Food Prospects and Policies*, Brookings Institution, Washington, DC, 1978

——, 'The Role of International Trade in Solving the Food Problems of the Developing Countries', in International Food Policy Issues: A Proceedings USDA Foreign Agricultural Economics Report No. 143, Washington, DC, January 1978

Sarris, A.H. and Taylor, L., 'Cereal Stocks. Food Aid and Food Security for the Poor' in Bhagwati, J., *The New International Economic Order: The North South Debate*, MIT Press, Cambridge, Mass., 1977

Scobie, G., *Government Policy and Food Imports — The Case of Egypt*, IFPRI, December 1981

Sharples, Jerry A., *An Evaluation of US Grain Reserve Policy 1977–80*, USDA Econ Research Service, Agricultural Economic Report No. 4, 1981

Siamwalla, Ammar and Haykin, Stephen, *The World Rice Market, Structure, Conduct and Performance*, IFPRI Research Report 39, Washington, DC, 1983

Sinha, Radha, *The World Food Problem: Consensus and Conflict*, Pergamon Press, New York, 1978

Stone, Bruce, *A Review of Chinese Agricultural Statistics 1949–79*, IFPRI Research Report 16, Washington, DC, 1980

Strak, J., *Measurement of Agricultural Protection*, Macmillan/Trade Policy Research Centre, London, 1982

Talbot, R., *The Chicken War*, Iowa State University Press, Ames, Iowa, 1978

Tang, Anthony M. and Stone, Bruce, *Food Production in the People's Republic of*

China, IFPRI Research Report 15, Washington, DC, 1980

Tarrant, J.R., *Food Policies*, Wiley, New York, 1980

Timmer, C.P., *The Political Economy of Rice in Asia*, Food Research Institute, Stamford, 1976

Timmer, C. Peter, Falcon, W.P. and Pearson, S.R., *Food Policy Analysis*, Johns Hopkins UP/World Bank, Washington, DC, 1983

Timmer, C. Peter, 'China and the World Food System' in Goldberg, R.A. (ed.) *Research in Domestic and International Agribusiness Management*, Jai Press, Greenwich, Connecticut, 1981

Tracy, M., *Agriculture in Western Europe: Challenge and Response 1880–1980* (2nd edn), Granada, London, 1982

Tracy, M. and Hodac, I., *Prospects for Agriculture in the European Economic Community*, College of Europe/De Tempel, Bruges, 1979

Trager, J., *The Great Grain Robbery*, Ballentine, New York, 1975

Tweeten, Luther, *Foundations of US Farm Policy*, University of Nebraska Press, 1979

Underwood, John M., *Food Security and Food Policy in a World of Uncertainty*, Rockefeller Foundation, USA, 1979

US Central Intelligence Agency, *Potential Implications of Trends in World Population, Food Production and Climate*, CIA, OPR 401, 1974

US Congress, House Committee on International Relations, *Use of Food Resources for Diplomatic Purposes — An Examination of the Issues*, Congressional Research Service Library of Congress, Committee Print HD 9002, Washington, DC, 1977

US Department of Agriculture, *Agricultural Food Policy Review Perspectives for the 1980s*, Economics and Statistics Service, USDA, Washington, DC, April 1981

——, *Another Revolution in US Farming*, USDA, Washington, DC, 1979

——, *World Grain Situation and Outlook*, annual, USDA, Washington, DC, various years

US Department of Agriculture Economic Research Service, *Situation and Outlook Reports for Individual Regions including Western Europe, USSR, China and Southeast Asia*, annual

US General Accounting Office, *Grain Reserves: A Potential US Food Policy Tool*, US Government, Washington DC, 1976

US Senate Committee on Agriculture, Nutrition and Forestry, *Farm Structure: An Historical Perspective on Changes in the Number and Size of Farms*, Government Printing Office, Washington, DC, 1980

US Senate Committee on Banking, Housing and Urban Affairs, *Suspension of US Exports of High Technology and Grain to the Soviet Union*, US Government Printing Office, Washington, DC, 1980

US Senate Committee on Finance, International Trade Sub-Committee, *European Communities' CAP, The Subsidies Code and Enforcement of US Rights Under Trade Agreement*, US Government Printing Office, Washington, DC, 1982

——, *Problems in International Agricultural Trade*, US Government, Washington, DC, July 1977

US Senate Committee on Foreign Relations, *Multinationals and US Foreign Policy: The International Grain Companies*, US Government, June 1978

Valdes, Alberto, *Food Security for Developing Countries*, Westview, Boulder, Colorado, 1981

——, *Trade Liberalisation in Agricultural Commodities and the Potential Foreign Exchange Benefits to Developing Countries*, Washington, DC, International Food Policy Research Institute, 1979

Valdes, Alberto and Zietz, Joachim, *Agricultural Protection in OECD Countries: Its*

Cost to Less Developed Countries, IFPRI Research Report 21, Washington, DC, 1980

Vitanova, G., *Trade Prospects for Centrally Planned Economies*, Agriculture Canada, 1982

Voskresensky, Lev, *Food Programme: Its Aim*, Novosti Press Agency, Moscow, 1982

Wallace, W., *Britain in Europe*, Heinemann, London, 1982

Wallerstein, Mitchel, *Food for War, Food for Peace: United States Food Aid in a Global Context*, MIT Press, Cambridge, Mass., 1980

Warley, T.K., 'Western Trade in Farm Products' in *International Economic Relations of the Western World. 1959–71*, ed. Shonfield, London, Oxford University Press, 1976

World Bank, *World Development Report*, various issues, World Bank, Washington, DC, various years

Yudelman, M., *Development Issues in the 80s: Achieving Food Security*, Paper presented at 26th Annual Conference of the Australian Agricultural Economics Society, Melbourne, February 1982

INDEX